Buffalo Gal

"This book is compulsively readable, and owes its deadpan delivery to the fact that she has performed standup comedy on national television (*The Oprah Winfrey Show, Late Night with David Letterman, Today, Primetime*, etc.)."

—*ForeWord* Magazine

Best Bet

"The book's laugh-out-loud funny, and readers will find themselves rereading lines just for the sheer joy of it."

—*Kirkus Reviews*

The Big Shuffle

"Although it's a laugh-out-loud read, it's an appealing, sensitive, superbly written book. One you won't want to put down. I loved it."

—*The Lakeland Times*

"Be prepared to fall in love with a story as wise as it is witty."

—*The Compulsive Reader*

The Sweetest Hours

"To call *The Sweetest Hours* a book of short stories would be like calling the *Mona Lisa* a painting."

—*Front Street Reviews*

"Pedersen weaves tales that blend humor, sorrow, and sometimes surprise endings in the games of life and love."

—*Book Loons*

Heart's Desire

"Funny, tender, and poignant, *Heart's Desire*
should appeal to a wide range of readers."

—*Booklist*

"Prepare to fall in love again because Laura Pedersen is giving
you your 'Heart's Desire' by bringing back Hallie Palmer and
her entire endearing crew. In a story as wise as it is witty,
Pedersen captures the joy of love found, the ache of love lost,
and how friends can get you through it all—win or lose."

—Sarah Bird, author of *The Yokota Officers Club*

"This book will make you laugh and cry and like a good friend,
you'll be happy to have made its acquaintance."

—Lorna Landvik, author of
Angry Housewives Eating Bon Bons

Last Call

"Pedersen writes vividly of characters so interesting, so funny
and warm that they defy staying on the page."

—*The Hartford Courant*

"This book is a rare, humorous exploration of death
that affirms life is a gift and tomorrow is never guaranteed.
Pedersen writes an exquisitely emotional story.
A must-have book to start the new year."

—*Romantic Times*

Beginner's Luck

"Laura Pedersen delivers…if this book hasn't been made into
a screenplay already, it should be soon. Throughout, you can't
help but think how hilarious some of the scenes would play on
the big screen."

—*The Hartford Courant*

"Funny, sweet-natured, and well-crafted...Pedersen has created a wonderful assemblage of...whimsical characters and charm."
— *Kirkus Reviews*

"This novel is funny and just quirky enough to become a word-of-mouth favorite...Pedersen has a knack for capturing tart teenage observations in witty asides, and Hallie's naiveté, combined with her gambling and numbers savvy, make her a winning protagonist."
— *Publishers Weekly*

"A breezy coming-of-age novel with an appealing cast of characters."
— *Booklist*

Going Away Party

"Pedersen shows off her verbal buoyancy. Their quips are witty and so are Pedersen's amusing characterizations of the eccentric MacGuires. Sentence by sentence, Pedersen's debut can certainly entertain."
— *Publishers Weekly*

Play Money

"A savvy insider's vastly entertaining line on aspects of the money game."
— *Kirkus Reviews* (starred review)

Also by Laura Pedersen

LauraPedersenBooks.com

Planes, Trains,
and Auto-Rickshaws

A Journey through Modern India

Laura
Pedersen

FULCRUM

GOLDEN, COLORADO

Text © 2012 Laura Pedersen

Library of Congress Cataloging-in-Publication Data
Pedersen, Laura.
    Planes, trains, and auto-rickshaws : a journey through modern India / Laura Pedersen.
        p. cm.
    ISBN 978-1-55591-618-3 (pbk.)
1. India--Description and travel. 2. Pedersen, Laura--Travel--India. 3. India--Social life and customs. 4. Women--India--Social conditions. 5. Children--India--Social conditions. 6. India--Social conditions--1947- I. Title.
    DS414.2.P43 2012
    915.404'532--dc23

                                  2012005900

Printed in Canada
0 9 8 7 6 5 4 3 2 1

Design by Jack Lenzo

Fulcrum Publishing
4690 Table Mountain Dr., Ste. 100
Golden, CO 80403
800-992-2908 • 303-277-1623
www.fulcrumbooks.com

In memory of Nina Kohnstamm (1940–2011)—
teacher, traveler, friend

Contents

Bewildered, Bothered, and Bewitched

My introduction to India came through that bedrock of American recreation during the latter half of the twentieth century, the television. Specifically, the 1960s sitcom. *Bewitched* starred the stunning, nose-twitching actress Elizabeth Montgomery as Samantha Stephens, a good witch who decided to forego her magical powers (most of the time) in order to achieve the 1960s version of the female American Dream as an average suburban housewife. However, when otherworldly symptoms arose, more often than not caused by the bumbling Aunt Clara and her spells gone bad, it was necessary to call on the family witch doctor, Dr. Bombay. Thereby my first association with all things India at the impressionable age of five was in the form of Welsh-born character actor Bernard Fox, appearing out of thin air dressed in outlandish costumes, surrounded by a coterie of sexy nurses, cracking corny jokes, and providing questionable cures.

India next appeared when I started kindergarten, in 1970. There weren't any students who hailed from the subcontinent in my Western New York elementary school, but American Indians were going from being called *Indians* to *Native Americans*, except by actual Native Americans who, by and large, preferred being called Indians. So when someone said the word *Indian*, kids often asked, "Dot or feather?" This was just before political correctness came into being (Need any Helen Keller jokes?).

However, such nomenclature confusion existed for good reason. *Indian* was the name Christopher Columbus (the Italian who got funding from Spain to discover a country that would be taken over by England, only to gain independence with help from France) gave the people he found in the New World, believing he'd arrived in the Indies, which was the medieval name for Asia. To further befuddle things, islands in the Caribbean Sea came to be called the West Indies when it turned out they weren't the Indies of the East. And, just for fun, the islands known as the Lesser Antilles are located in the eastern West Indies.

In the neighborhood where I grew up, people regularly headed off to play bingo at the Seneca Indian Reservation or the neighborhood Catholic church, despite the Corinthians 1:36 edict against ill-gotten gains. The Seneca Reservation had the advantage of tax-free gas and cigarettes, while the church offered nonalcoholic refreshments and guilt. In the 1980s and '90s, American Indian tribes around the country were busy expanding their gambling enterprises by building actual casinos with hotels and stage shows. Meantime, India Indians in America were taking over 7-Elevens, Carvel stores, and roadside motels at a rate that provided a gold mine of material for stand-up comics—the likes of which wouldn't be seen again until Vice President Dick Cheney accidentally shot his hunting partner in the face and Osama Bin Laden was found to have more pornography than Times Square in the 1970s.

Technology began booming in the 1980s and the subcontinent soon became known for operating call centers, where your service inquiries would be routed, especially for operational issues, such as whether your CD–ROM drive could interchangeably hold a disc or a coffee cup (Answer: no). As a result, by the time I arrived on Wall Street and the word *Indian* came up, colleagues asked, "Computer or casino?" Political correctness was late in hitting the stock exchange, as evidenced by the weekly bimbo contests in which traders competed to see how many scantily clad women could be lured to the trading floor for "free tours" that ended on a balcony with a Plexiglas barrier that transformed pantygazing from a sport into a vocation for hundreds of male employees.

I'd wanted to travel to India for many years but feared that the poverty and misogyny would be too disquieting. I had read articles about children purposely maimed to beg more efficiently and wives cast out of their husband's homes after mysterious cooking accidents and forced to live on the streets scarred and deformed, if they survived at all. Meantime, the stories went on, if a woman's husband happened to die, she suddenly found herself in terrible circumstances. And women in bad marriages regularly resorted to suicide rather than apply for divorce because of the social stigma. Having been raised as a Unitarian Universalist during the 1970s, when the opportunities for women in this country were still largely limited to housewife, teacher, nurse, or Miss America, I spent many weekends marching to support equal rights for women while my dad enjoyed pointing out that our local feminist collective bookstore contained no humor section. So I secretly worried that upon entering the country I'd have flashbacks complete with a Helen Reddy soundtrack, dash into the first Indian women and children's advocacy group I came across, and devote the rest of my days to folding pamphlets, building birthing centers, and promoting the serious business of *change*.

However, by the start of the new millenium, surveys were confirming that the recent success of the Indian economy was partly due to the fact that women had finally been given the freedom to fully participate in this surging democracy. Their contributions, from piecemeal worker all the way up to president, were a substantial component in powering an economic engine with a 9 percent growth rate and the potential to lift millions out of poverty. When women were no longer discriminated against or treated as encumbrances, but given opportunity, they quickly became society's biggest assets. This was something worth seeing.

Another factor that had been holding me back was that the land of swamis, meditation, yoga, toe rings, and walking barefoot on fire was also renowned for mob violence. When two Sikh bodyguards gunned down prime minister Indira Gandhi in 1984, more than three thousand citizens were killed during the frenzied days that followed. In 2002, a train fire that killed fifty-eight passengers, mostly Hindu pilgrims, was blamed on Muslims, and more than two thousand died in the riotous aftermath; people were burned alive, women and young girls were raped while government officials looked the other way, and two hundred thousand Muslims were driven from their homes. On a lesser but still worrisome note, when a popular 1980s Indian television serialization of the religious epic Ramayana came to an end, viewers took to the streets with bricks and bottle rockets in a region that was home to some particularly dedicated and hotheaded audience members. Would the safety-conscious traveler need also to carry a TV guide?

Lastly, when it came to corndog-fed foreigners, the food and water in India had a reputation for being a dysentery delivery system that resulted in what we called the crabapple two-step back home in Western New York.

Obviously the United States has its fair share of problems, but at least here I could vote, protest, and volunteer and thereby feel that I'm at least attempting to make some small contribution to improving my corner of the world. In India, I'd be nothing more than a helpless observer.

However, by 2010 I wasn't getting any younger. I'd survived disco, Afros, Pintos, *Jaws*, Oddjob, atomic wedgies, rainbow wedgies, and Watergate. I went to school back when trophies were handed out for *winning,* not participation. I was on my sixth dog, to be exact, and reports from the subcontinent suggested that things were changing for the better. Furthermore, India was one of the few countries in that part of the world where citizens didn't hate the United States like it was a job they were getting paid to perform. After trips to Greece, Russia, and Egypt, I was tired of pretending to be Canadian, which entailed keeping up with hockey scores and memorizing recipes for making peameal back bacon.

My divorced parents, after having both lost their spouses within the space of fourteen months, seemed to be getting back on track as best they could. At least they appeared healthy—Mom solicited actual doctors' opinions, and you just sort of eyeballed Dad to make sure he was getting his daily allowance of coffee, cigarettes, Corona, and pastrami, since he's a man at two with nature. As an only child, it occurred to me that some energetic younger brothers and sisters might come in handy, especially since Mom and Dad were living two thousand miles apart. Unfortunately, when you advertise for siblings on Craigslist at this age and stage, consumers are more interested in your potential as an organ donor than as a big sister.

Eastward Ho!

Two days day after buying my ticket on the state-owned Air India, direct from New York to New Delhi, the airline experienced a horrible crash that killed 158 people. A plane coming from Dubai overshot a runway in southern India, hurtled into a ravine, and exploded. My travel agent e-mailed: But that was their first accident in ten years—*Freakonomics* would tell us that the odds say you are safer on them after an accident because they are not "due" for another ten years!! Or you now prefer I explore connecting options?

Her logic was compelling—until you factored in that the cause of the crash was poor pilot training and tricky landing facilities. But the meandering cloud of volcanic ash tap-dancing its way across Europe like crickets on a hot stove still made a direct flight preferable, so I threw caution to the wind the way one does when climbing aboard Coney Island's rackety Cyclone roller coaster. Air India it was. The key to a brilliant vacation is finding adventure and possibility in the face of disaster and tragedy. And a prescription for Ambien.

By catching a cab from Manhattan to JFK

Airport, in Queens, you already feel that you're half-way to Southeast Asia, since most drivers in Manhattan hail from India, Pakistan, or Bangladesh, and they jabber away in their singsong native tongues on hands-free cell phones while attempting to break the taxi land speed record. These phone calls entail multiple listeners, so a driver can apparently have his entire extended family of six hundred on the line at once to discuss who's bringing the rasam masala to the Friday night mosque social. The constantly under construction JFK Airport, with its outdated facilities, poor signage, sickly fluorescent lighting, and flock of live-in birds, operates much like a developing country, so this furthers a smooth transition.

I arrived at the airport just twenty-four hours after fed-up flight attendant Steven Slater performed a spectacular "take this job and shove it" on the JFK tarmac subsequent to being cursed out by a defiant passenger. He grabbed a couple beers, disembarked on the inflatable emergency evacuation slide with one in each hand, dashed to the employee parking lot, and headed home, where he was promptly arrested for reckless endangerment and criminal mischief. *The Washington Post* dubbed it "pulling a Slater," perhaps to suggest a nonviolent version of "going postal." I felt everyone's pain—passengers, pilots, and flight attendants alike. The tarmac at JFK is an enormous parking lot where one spends mind-numbing hours waiting to take off amidst the sound of jackhammers and strange smells that, best I can tell, involve past-its-prime egg salad. Or else one waits for a gate to open up following a long flight while babies cry and toilets overflow and people are famished for anything but a minipretzel. New Yorkers know that rules about remaining in their seats don't apply to them. What are the airport police going to do—take away our feet?

Surely there will soon be an annual awards ceremony for individuals who go berserk in the most newsworthy way, such as when a cell phone rang nonstop during a one-woman off-Broadway show. When the theatergoer finally answered, the actress hopped offstage, got on the line, and explained the circumstances to the caller. How many actors can say they've received a standing ovation just ten minutes into a performance?

I haven't yet turned into a cell phone freak, but sadly I have become one of those people who arrive for long international flights wearing pajamas. I vaguely recall that when I was a child, people actually used to dress up for plane travel as if they were going to a wife-swapping party. That was back before passengers were required to strip, have their skivvies wanded, and submit to a colonoscopy prior to boarding.

Nowadays many people wear their sweats and scuffs to the airport like toddlers being taken to a drive-in movie. It's hard to blame frequent fliers, since they know what it's like to spend several days waiting out a power failure, terrorist attack, or volcano eruption while sleeping atop molded plastic chairs and bathing in the shallow metal sink of a public restroom. And just when that ordeal ends, reclaiming one's luggage is more like awaiting the birth of a first child. That's why a sequined poly-blend tracksuit has come to symbolize what naturalists call adaptability and functions as the linchpin to our survival as a species. Or as Gilbert and Sullivan so memorably wrote: "Let the punishment fit the crime." Next stop, New Delhi.

Planes, Trains, and Auto-Rickshaws

I discovered that catching a cab from the airport to your hotel in any Indian metropolis is an exercise in patience and networking, as would seem to be the case throughout much of Eastern Europe and the Middle East. You will *see* lots of taxis, but whenever you inquire about hiring one, a man leads you in the opposite direction. A transaction may eventually occur that appears to be on the up-and-up, but you still don't climb into a cab. Noisy caucusing continues at curbside or in a parking lot as if political candidates are being selected in some smoke-filled back room. There are more conversations and peregrinations, and finally you're excited to be loading your bags into a trunk. However, the driver now disappears for a period of time. Several people have asked you for money "for helping," which is a good moment to point out that you requested a taxi and not to be led through a labyrinth of wheeler-dealers who appear to have been extras in *Slumdog Million-aire*. The driver then returns with someone else who has also been "helped." On the bright side, using the pre-paid taxi stand (which does not cut out nearly as many middlemen as one would think) avoids any unexpected companions and tours of the city that serve to run up the meter. However, the only place I've seen more hot meters than in New York City is Bulgaria, where the taxis are driven by former Olympic weightlifters and thus negotiation is discouraged.

The real culture shock of New Delhi doesn't begin so much with the separate exit from baggage claim for ladies as it does upon hitting the highway. You're driving in a country where one hundred thousand people a year are killed in road accidents, which would be like losing the entire population of Boulder, Colorado, by the end of every December. The city of Delhi alone has about ten thousand accidents a year, with twenty-five hundred fatalities. And this is a place without blizzards, black ice, or avalanches. Driver's education clearly needs to be supplemented with classes in applied physics, because the main problem is that the roads are filled with a wide range of objects of varying weights, number of legs, and trajectories traveling at different velocities, including but not confined to: pedestrians, pedicabs, pushcarts, rickshaws, auto-rickshaws, bicycle rickshaws, scooters, careening motorcycles, antique tractors, heavy machinery, brightly painted trucks, buses, cars, thirty-year-old Fiat taxis, SUVs, donkey carts, oxen, bovines, goats, and equal numbers of three- and four-legged dogs. My favorites were the makeshift vehicles constructed from the leftover parts of others (presumably demolished in accidents), such as a combine seat and steering wheel atop a minivan chassis with the windshield of an old crop duster and the bell from a bicycle. Think *Chitty Chitty Bang Bang*. None of these modes of conveyance contained seatbelts or airbags (unless you include animal bladders). Anything framed in metal featured numerous dents, while anything framed in fur sported bald spots. Two questions immediately arose: (1) Is my life insurance paid up? and (2) Where are all the trial lawyers?

Did I mention the marching bands and parade floats? Even if you don't get invited to an Indian wedding (which can last a week and would probably take up your entire trip anyway), you might still participate in one, as the festivities normally gravitate toward the streets at a certain point, and on some nights two or three celebratory caravans roar past with music blaring, intoxicated revelers dancing, and the turbaned groom riding atop a blinged-out elephant or white horse. Which brings me to the only roadside installations I expected to see but didn't—Motel 6, Carvel, and 7-Eleven.

"There are no bad drivers in Manhattan," goes the old joke, "because they're all dead." This is far from the case in India. Most driving is done with the horn. Although another clear-cut rule seems to be "When in doubt, shout." As for lanes, there aren't any to speak of on these lunar-cratered roads, not between vehicles going the same way or to separate traffic headed in opposite directions. There are no shoulders alongside the roads. There are few traffic lights (that work) or signs or other legal impediments to moving at top speed. The written portion of the Indian licensing exam must be incredibly short. Some busy urban intersections feature a traffic cop, but he often gets into long conversations or conflagrations with pedestrians, and thus continues an endless high-speed game of horn-honking chicken. Because whenever any of the aforementioned modes of transport give way, drivers hit their accelerators as if fleeing a crime scene.

The best strategy to avoid crashing into another vehicle is apparently for the driver not to acknowledge that it exists, which is easily accomplished by not looking left, right, or in the rearview mirror (if there is one) and ignoring the outsized horn section of the automotive orchestra. Oddly, most trucks and buses don't have bumper stickers saying "I Brake for Animals" or "Vishnu Is the Answer" but rather "Horn OK Please" or "Blow Horn," which seems like an invitation to trouble. However, if you wish to pass a large vehicle on a narrow road, you really are supposed to honk, and people do a lot of it. One is left to speculate whether musical air horns playing the pulse-pounding Hindi hit songs "Kabootar Ja, Ja, Ja" or "Khamosh Hai Zamana" would make things better or worse.

On Indian roads, larger vehicles always have the right of way, similar to how in a Buffalo blizzard the least expensive jalopy is entitled to go first solely because the Mercedes driver prefers not to be smashed to bits. The exceptions are that, technically speaking, a motorbike is larger than a goat and a car is larger than a cow, however, goats and cows do not have steering and thus have the right of way.

In case you suspect this contains the slightest bit of exaggeration, let the record show that when the popular TV show *Ice Road Truckers* created a new spin-off called *IRT: Deadliest Roads*, the first stop was India. Furthermore, the three *veterans* of the show, driving wood-framed cement-loaded rigs from Delhi to the Himalayas, were either terrific actors or completely petrified for their lives. Apparently the treacherous roads of northern Alaska are nothing next to this death-defying automotive extravaganza. Or as the circus proprietor who encounters a pushmi-pullyu in the musical *Doctor Dolittle* exclaims, "I've never seen anything like it in all my life!"

Hopefully you'll manage to avoid any road collisions, but be prepared for some pedestrian run-ins. The fact that Indians drive on the left has unintended consequences for walking Westerners since we tend to veer right to pass, while Indians automatically go left. Attention women: high heels, open-toe sandals, jellies, and flip-flops are *not* recommended footwear.

For some reason, I assumed that traveling from Manhattan to Delhi for the first time would be like moving from the Buffalo suburbs to the heart of New York City in 1983, when I was eighteen. The city was just crawling out of its *Mean Streets* chain-snatching, token-sucking, muggin' and druggin', homicidal maniac, squeegee men days, and people were shocked that I'd leave a city with a high suicide rate for one with an even higher homicide rate. Why trade snowstorms for serial killers? Avenues teemed with hurried and harried pedestrians, graffiti-covered subways greeted passengers with ear-piercing brake squeals and unintelligible announcements while rodents freely plied their trade far from Habitrails. Street preachers with ZZ Top beards shouted apocalyptic pronouncements up and down Broadway while brightly costumed fortune tellers separated tourists from their money on the cracked sidewalks of Greenwich Village. My second day in town, a woman standing behind me in a New York University lecture hall announced that she couldn't sit down because of hemorrhoids. That would have been more than enough information right there. But no, she had to add that these hemorrhoids were the result of "pushing too hard." Sensory overload. Since we were in an educational environment, she apparently assumed this was a teachable moment and concluded with, "So be careful."

Alone in the bustling capital city of Delhi, I reminded myself of all the things I'd learned, sometimes the hard way, about city living: don't trust anyone on the street, be assertive, even aggressive, and act a little loco if necessary. Remaining vigilant had also served me in good stead during recent trips to Cairo, Istanbul, and Casablanca, all heaving metropolises filled with entrepreneurs overly anxious for tourist trade, where Westerners are constantly harassed to hire guides and are held hostage over cups of tea in rug shops. If you're a woman traveling solo, it becomes annoying to the point that you can no longer enjoy taking in the sights as a pedestrian. Eventually, you may even long for Athens, where public square dwellers laboring as unpaid critics remove the cigarettes from their lips just long enough to scowl at American tourists.

But none of this defensive behavior was necessary. Even the de rigueur cab-driver shuffle was performed in lilting voices with smiles and friendliness. People in Delhi seemed for the most part purposeful, heading to work and school or busy operating their outdoor stalls. Locals are polite and helpful if you need something and leave you be if you don't. Few police officers carry guns. And most criminals don't carry firearms. The joke is that lawbreakers are much better off approaching the police with hard cash rather than handguns. This is so different from Manhattan, where no one pulls out a gun, because chances are that everyone else has one too. I wasn't accosted by panhandlers or children who'd been blinded or maimed in order

to become more effective beggars. Pimps weren't pros-
tituting women in alleyways. I didn't even see a car
with a sign saying "Radio Already Stolen," which never
seems to go out of style on my street back home, where
ear-piercing car alarms serve as the city's theme song.

Mother India

I arrived the night before Independence Day. On August 15, 1947, India threw off the shackles following 347 years of British rule and declared itself a sovereign nation where every man and woman would have a vote. Actually, that was the plan, but at the last minute, an astrologer came dashing in with charts fluttering and declared that August 15 was bad luck, and they moved things back to midnight of the 14th so no one would be struck by lightning. Independence Day in India is a somewhat staid affair, with the prime minister hoisting a flag from the ramparts of the historic Red Fort in New Delhi and giving a carefully crafted speech highlighting everything he's accomplished that year. At local cultural centers, schoolchildren sing patriotic songs and act out the roles of main players in the revolution, such as Mahatma Gandhi and Jawaharlal Nehru. Then everyone heads home to watch *Indian Idol*, the top-rated TV show.

Sadly missing were backyard barbecues, small-town parades, three-legged races, hot dog–eating contests, fireworks, M-80s tossed into backyards, potato salad left in the sun too long, bonfires built too close to garages, and the obligatory trips to the emergency room. But that's understandable, since the Islamic Republic of Pakistan was carved out on the same day, which resulted in massacres of entire villages along with the largest human migration in history. Hindus and Sikhs moved south and east to India, while Muslims headed north and west for Pakistan, making a grand total of about 12 million displaced persons. It didn't help that in order to maintain control of India, the Brits had played the Hindus and Muslims against each other for decades, so there was already a substantial amount of ill will brewing. The consequence was that more than a million people lost their lives during the violent and bloody chaos known as Partition.

Although Independence Day isn't the exuberant celebration to which Americans are accustomed, fireworks come out in full force during Diwali, the Hindu Festival of Lights, which usually occurs in November or December, depending on the position of the moon. Diwali commemorates the return of Lord Rama from exile, proclaims the triumph of good over evil, and marks the Hindu New Year. This five-day celebration entails full-scale merrymaking and falls during the tourist season (October through May) rather than monsoon season (June through September). And the springtime festival of Holi, which involves throwing buckets of colored powder and colored water at friends, family, and strangers, gives the appearance of fireworks having been unleashed at ground level.

There appear to be as many festivals in India as there are gods and goddesses. In Bollywood movies, it's always at a festival where the protagonist loses his twin brother or sister. When traveling through the subcontinent, Mark Twain noted that although a week has only seven days, Indians seemed to celebrate eight festivals every week. They run the gamut from the religious and political to the agricultural and commercial. There are gala events to celebrate elephants, chariots, mangoes, monsoons, full moons, and even inner light. One festival involves hurling paint at people and another features body piercing. A ten-day-long celebration in October commemorates the slaying of the buffalo-headed demon Mahishasura by Durga, wife of the god Shiva. People blow sacred conch shells, offer prayers, and shower enormous statues of the Hindu goddess with countless marigolds. One must assume that schoolchildren don't get every holiday off, or they'd be in class only four days out of the entire year.

Marijuana smoking is especially popular at holy festivals. Technically speaking, cannabis is illegal in most parts of India, but busting potheads isn't high on police officers' to-do lists in what is sometimes referred to as a functional anarchy. Just be careful about where you decide to take a stoner nap, since India is the hair export capital of the world, and while tresses are usually harvested through consensual head shaving at temples (a form of sacrifice), your lustrous ponytail might suddenly be snipped off by a hair robber after your consciousness has been sufficiently raised or lowered.

British rule over India was known as the Raj, a Hindi word from the Sanskrit *raja*, which means "king." India was declared "The Jewel in the Crown" of the British Empire for being its most valuable colony, with a wealth of natural resources that included diamonds, raw cotton, wheat, tea, coffee, jute (a plant fiber used to make twine), burlap, and cheap paper. Also, the country's outsized population could be made to pay tariffs that would fill the royal coffers. I recall something from a fourth-grade history class about American colonists eventually getting slightly ticked about a similar taxation without representation situation.

Prior to British reign, India was a vast array of competing kingdoms that occasionally invaded and took over one another, not unlike a giant game of Risk. Following independence, the various maharajas, which is Sanskrit for "great kings," were given a stipend from the government but no longer had administrative powers or the authority to collect taxes. By the early 1970s, all of their privileges had been ended and their titles revoked. They are now, technically speaking, "former maharaja so-and-so," similar to how the recording star who changed his name to an unpronounceable symbol was for years called The Artist Formerly Known as Prince.

Several of the maharajas' palaces still stand and can be visited, while a few have been turned into hotels. Much like how Sitting Bull joined William F. Cody's Wild West Show after the whole America thing didn't work out as planned, a number of maharajas along with their offspring entered the tourist trade and now offer grandiose accommodation in former palaces, complete with billiards rooms, heated swimming pools, tea and cucumber sandwiches alongside the croquet lawn, spas offering Ayurvedic massage, and ancestral portrait galleries featuring portly men with impressive handlebar mustaches and intelligent dark eyes beneath brilliantly jeweled turbans.

Today, with 1.2 billion people, India is the world's largest democracy and the second most populous country after China. There isn't a national language but rather an official language, which is Hindi. (Hindi is the more proper version of the language spoken by politicians and newscasters, while Hindustani is the less rigid form heard in the streets and chai stalls.) English is the second official language, so it's easy to follow street signs, make reservations, purchase tickets, and communicate with hospitality workers, who almost all speak English. Furthermore, because Hindi is mostly spoken in the north, English is used to connect north and south. Most Indians know at least two languages, and educated Indians are often fluent in three or four or five languages. States are allowed to operate in their native tongues, so all in all you have twenty-two government-recognized languages with people speaking in more than two hundred variations and dialects. It can be difficult for English speakers to pronounce Hindi and trying out a few phrases will more likely result in widespread amusement than create a positive impression. But if you do manage to say something vaguely comprehensible, Indians will be astounded, flattered, and thrilled and want to take you home for dinner and show you off to their entire family.

Indians are naturally loquacious, so I found it easy to strike up extended casual conversations and was not surprised to learn that they have the longest constitution in the world (which went into effect January 26, 1950). The musically accented Indian voice sounds perennially cheerful, and I'm not sure how you'd know if a local was really frustrated with you. But such widespread comprehension of English aids the current economic liftoff and keeps tourism robust. Indians are as creative with their speech as they are in business. Vishal Nagar, a concierge at the Hyatt Regency in Delhi, produced a word new to my ears, *prepone*. If you want to defer an appointment, then obviously you postpone it; but if you want to bring something forward and make it earlier, then Mr. Nagar is happy to prepone the activity for you. Meantime, if you want to enter a building from the rear, you'll be going in through its *backside*, and *denting* is used to describe the act of removing a dent from your car. Otherwise, Indians don't like to disappoint, and instead of saying no, they often nod agreeably while being vague about the details.

Old and New Delhi

India, which appears on the map as a huge inverted triangle with the Arabian Sea to the west and the Bay of Bengal to the east, was one of the cradles of civilization along with Egypt and Mesopotamia. Delhi is the second largest metropolis after Mumbai. This five-hundred-square-mile area of northern India has been constantly inhabited since at least the sixth century BCE, the result of being strategically located on trade routes running from Egypt and Persia to China and Java. Consequently, the city is an architecture lover's dream, with over a thousand historic buildings still in existence.

Delhi is also famous for having been ruled by a woman, Razia al-Din, from 1236 to 1240, making her one of the few female sovereigns in Islamic history. She favored men's clothing and would lead her army into battle riding atop an elephant, without covering her face, which was considered pretty outrageous for the time. Razia established schools, research centers, and public libraries and allowed academic works by Hindus to be studied along with those by Muslims. Best of all, Razia would answer only to "Sultan," since

"Sultana" meant that one was the wife or mistress of a sultan. There's plenty of controversy with regard to how Razia died and where she was buried, but as one of the region's few female monarchs, she continues to be a rich subject for academics, writers, and filmmakers.

New Delhi is the current capital and makes up one of nine districts of the area known as Delhi but remains a separate territory similar to Washington, DC, in America and Canberra in Australia. The city was designed by famous British architects Sir Edwin Lutyens and Sir Herbert Baker and is known for its sixty miles of wide, straight, tree-lined boulevards, villas with landscaped gardens, mixture of styles, and overall grandiosity. Begun in 1911, the new capital was meant to be elegant and impressive in contrast to the crowded alleyways, chaotic bazaars, and makeshift housing of Old Delhi, and also to let the Indians know who was in charge. The sprawling Viceroy Palace (also called the Rashtrapati Bhawan), with its six miles of corridors and 340 rooms, is larger than the Palace of Versailles, in France. Standing atop Raisina Hill, with a great copper dome 180 feet high and massive sec- retariat and legislature buildings on either side, the palace is probably India's best known monument after the Taj Mahal and Qutub Minar. It was completed in 1931 for a grand total of $10 million, just sixteen years before the British would end its dominion over the subcontinent once and for all.

During the three and a half centuries the British ruled India, they transformed its appearance, institutions, and culture. Up went universities, city halls, museums, stately homes, barracks, private clubs, public libraries, and schools, all connected by a network of roads, railways, canals, and bridges. The telegraph was introduced, along with an efficient postal system and, eventually, hydroelectric power. The British, of course, ushered in the game of cricket, which is to India today what hockey is to Canada and war is to the United States: the national sport. Ironically, the countrywide press created by the British became a primary vehicle for Indians to express their displeasure with foreign rule and generate unrest. Partition was especially brutal on Delhi, with its close proximity to the border of Pakistan, and the population of the city doubled overnight with refugees, a shock of such magnitude that the area is still recovering sixty-five years later.

Along with imports of spice, silk, coffee, and tea from India, new words arrived on English shores—*verandah, avatar, cheroot, typhoon, bungalow, calico, cummerbund, dungarees, guru, juggernaut, jungle, karma, loot, pajamas, shampoo, ghoul,* and *thug.* A *jackal's wedding* meant "a sun shower." Foods such as chutney, curried eggs, and gingery puddings were introduced to the British diet. And in exchange for cricket, India gave her overlords the ultimate aristocratic game of polo, played with specially bred ponies on a manicured sward.

There were other cultural exchanges. Under the British raj, a number of reformers and missionaries' wives set up schools for the education and training of girls and crusaded not only for women's rights, but also to eliminate practices that did them direct harm, such as child marriage and banning widows from remarriage.

In the heart of New Delhi is the very Arc de Triomphe-ish granite and red sandstone India Gate, also designed by Lutyens, which was built as a memorial to the ninety thousand soldiers of the Indian Army who lost their lives fighting for the British Empire in World War I and the Third Anglo-Afghan War, in 1919 (Westerners have apparently been messing around in Afghanistan for a very long time). However, a statue of King George V was removed from the site following independence, and the gate has been subsequently rebranded as the Indian Army's Tomb of the Unknown Soldier.

The nearby Red Fort is India's architectural answer to Rome's Colosseum. This sprawling complex of palaces, pavilions, great halls, and gardens was constructed under emperor Shāh Jāhan in 1638 to house his royal family of the Peacock Throne and make sure the citizenry knew that someone powerfully important was in charge. Shāh Jāhan, the grandson of the legendary Akbar the Great, was a Mughal (also Mogul), an Indian Islamic dynasty that began ruling the subcontinent in the early 1500s and began losing power to the

British in the mid-1800s. The structures, which were once covered in gold and precious stones and inlaid with mosaics, are now crumbling, and some have been vandalized, but the fort is where India's flag was first raised and remains a powerful symbol of Indian sovereignty. It also does a first-rate job of showcasing a synthesis of Persian, European, and Indian architecture, with some whimsical touches resembling marzipan thrown in for good measure. At night, there's a sound and light show relating the history of the fort, which provides entertainment for tourists and a smooching opportunity for young people.

Across from the Red Fort is Jama Masjid, the largest mosque in India. Likewise built by Shāh Jāhan, Jama Masjid is a splendid example of Mughal style, with its three majestic black-and-white striped marble domes, three great gateways, four towers, two lofty minarets, and rectangular garden. It was finished in 1656, and thousands of Muslims continue to offer prayers there every day. Jama Masjid is located at the start of Delhi's famous Chandni Chowk, one of the country's oldest and busiest marketplaces, where you can find just about everything, from famous candy and tea shops, wood carvings, utensils, and specialty saris to currency traders, shrines, palaces, and police stations.

I found sightseeing in New and Old Delhi easy, interesting, and relaxed. Mosque visits require the removal of shoes, and women need to cover their heads and wear "modest dress." It's possible to borrow the necessary accoutrements before entering, but if you know in advance that you'll be mosquehopping, throw a shirt and headscarf into your bag. Modest dress means that arms and legs must be covered, and while it's fine for women to go around India in short-sleeved shirts, you probably don't want to strut about in shorts or a short skirt since some people might take offense. (In an effort to avoid mosquito bites, it's probably best to wear long pants, anyway.)

The soaring stone tower known as the Qutub Minar is the world's tallest brick minaret, and with its soaring spires and onion-shaped crowns, it's a wonderful example of Indo-Islamic architecture. A spiral staircase of 379 steps leads up to the balcony, and if that's not dizzying enough, the building is slightly tilted as a result of an earthquake. However, historians aren't sure exactly why the monument was built, therefore speculation abounds. One can assume the first Muslim sultan of India, Quṭb al-Dīn Aibak, who commissioned the tower, did not know that it would end up marked as a station on the yellow line of the Delhi Metro.

South Delhi is home to Lodi Gardens, a shady haven where Mughal tombs dating back to the fifteenth century decay amidst eucalyptus trees filled with colorful parrots and a popular place for jogging and morning walks. With a total of ninety acres, there's enough lawn space for tourists and locals to practice yoga and meditate without being disturbed by picnickers, cricketers, soccer players, or the spirits of those interred.

Just a few blocks away is the Indira Gandhi Memorial museum, the actual bungalow where the third prime minister lived and did much of her work, and the place she was assassinated. A mounted collection of photos recounts Indian history, and most of her personal effects are just as she left them. It's possible to see that the bindings on many of her books are cracked, suggesting that Ms. Gandhi actually read them. In the lush and otherwise tranquil gardens, a sculpted river of glass marks the spot where she was killed by her own bodyguards, on October 31, 1984.

For animal lovers, birders, and ornithologists, there's the Jain Bird Hospital in front of Red Fort. Veterinarians treat sick and wounded birds, which are then fed and cared for and given a safe haven to recover. The top floor houses hundreds of healed and happy birds waiting to be sprung, and the twice-a-month release is a touching, Disneylike sight. Most birds suffer injuries from the hazards of city living, but also as a result of run-ins with kites, as Delhi has many practitioners of this cutthroat sport. Birds are treated with the aim to release them into the wild, if that's where they came from. All comers are accepted, which is about three thousand birds at any given time, although half a dozen rabbits had managed to sneak in when I was there, and the proprietors say that down-on-their-luck squirrels are also admitted. There are no death panels operating here. The only way you won't get a big warm Jain welcome is if you're a carrion bird, since the pacifist Jains are also superstrict vegetarians. Because the bird hospital is part of a Digambar Jain temple, you must remove your shoes before entering, which is a little icky, but it's not as if you'll be stepping in bird poop or rabbit pellets—just walking on pavement. Workers are happy to give visitors a tour and donations are appreciated but not required.

While the bird hospital is uplifting, especially on release days, the Delhi Zoo is depressing. It's either woefully underfunded or else the money is being used to send its operators on Sri Lankan gambling junkets rather than care for the animals and maintain their habitats.

For lavatory lovers, there's the Sulabh International Museum of Toilets, which offers exhibits and information on twenty-five hundred years of, well, toilets. Considering the number of men I saw peeing along Delhi roadsides, this seems either ironic or redundant. But the truth is that 55 percent of the population do relieve themselves out of doors, and it's problematic for many reasons. Obviously, the spread of disease is a main concern, but since women have to go behind bushes for the sake of modesty, they run the risk of being bitten by snakes. Thus, proprietor Dr.

Bindeshwar Pathak is attempting to raise toilet awareness while helping experts in the field "learn from
the past and solve problems in the sanitation sector."
His Sulabh International Social Service Organization
has successfully placed more than 1.2 million toilets
around the country. However, if one is lucky enough
to have a toilet, it's important to follow the rules of
vastu shastra, a system of directional alignment, which
appears to be a Hindu version of feng shui and tells
you exactly where the toilet should be and what direction it should face for maximum results.

Foodies are in for a treat, as Delhi is rich in
North Indian cuisine, which tends to be a bit milder
than what you'll find in the spicier South, with its profusion of chili powder. *Chaat*, like tapas in Spain, is a
plate of savory snacks, though here they involve fried
dough, tangy chutneys, chickpeas, onion, coriander,
and yogurt, among other things. You can't have a wedding or a party without *chaat*. The popular *tikki ki
chaat* is like a South Asian version of a potato latke
and is available at restaurants, street stalls, and roadside carts. *Chaat* is often served on a dried banana leaf
that's been shaped into a bowl and thus is incredibly
environmentally friendly.

For the unadventurous eater, there's Pizza Hut,
Domino's, Papa John's, Subway, KFC, and McDon-
ald's (with locations in almost every Indian city). Since
Hindus don't eat beef, you won't find burgers at the

Golden Arches, but you can order the Maharaja Mac with pork or chicken or the vegetarian McAloo Tikki.

If you're concerned about becoming ill, then stay at a good hotel and order the pasta dish very hot. It's best to drink only sealed bottled water, but it can be hard to remember to use bottled water when brushing your teeth, which is also a good idea. And steer clear of any raw salads or sliced fruit that may have been sitting around collecting dysentery. For those intrigued by India's famous roadside food peddlers but circumspect about taking the plunge, it's possible to whip up your own *meethi lassi, bhel puri, paneer tikka*, masalas, chutneys, and samosas using the recipes in *Street Food of India* by Sephi Bergerson.

If you want to see India but you are freaking out about contracting the digestive distress commonly known as Delhi belly, pack some trail mix, PowerBars, pretzels, peanut butter, crackers, canned fish, chicken (or rice and beans), and Fig Newtons. Supplement this with washed and peeled local apples, pears, bananas, papaya, and lychee. Indian oranges aren't that flavorful compared to the ones Americans are accustomed to, but mangoes, when in season, are delicious. I've lived for weeks on this combo in a number of far-flung corners of the earth while heartier colleagues collapsed with food poisoning. It's a high-protein, low-fat diet that will have you returning home satisfied and slender. Therefore, don't skip the trip of a lifetime just because you're fearful of the food situation. I know a war correspondent who survived an entire year in Iraq eating only canned tuna that his mother sent from home.

Taj Mahal

No one should leave India without seeing the breath-takingly beautiful Taj Mahal, one of the seven wonders of the modern world (depending on the list). It is located in the city of Agra, about 120 miles south of New Delhi, and can be accomplished in a day trip. The train is your best bet, with the Taj Express or the Shatabdi Express leaving daily from Delhi's Hazrat Nizamuddin Station. However, you must book in advance. Most air-conditioned coach trips will make you a hostage to shopping stops, but if you like having a place to leave your belongings and don't mind browsing or waiting, then it's not so bad. Agra is a short hop by airplane. Traveling by car takes about three to six hours each way, depending on traffic, and will include several heart-pounding moments that may or may not end in a fiery death.

Note that the Taj Mahal is closed on Fridays. My guide said that it also used to be closed to foreigners on Mondays, because that day was set aside for Muslims as a free day of prayer and picnicking, but they left too many candy wrappers in the bushes, and so that was the end of that. Now it's open to the public on Mondays, despite what some older guidebooks might say.

The Taj Mahal, which was completed in 1653, is the most famous tomb in the world. The previously mentioned Mughal emperor Shāh Jāhan had it built in memory of his wife Mumtāz Mahal. The Taj is considered to be a monument to eternal love, since Mumtāz was the emperor's favorite wife, but I'm not sure that modern women equate endless love with being the darling out of a total of eight wives and dying while giving birth to one's fourteenth child. Still, the Taj is considered to be one of the most stunningly attractive buildings in the world, and on that it definitely delivers.

A Persian Muslim named Ustad Ahmad Lahauri is thought to have been the principal architect of the Taj Mahal, which took about twenty-two years to complete. The white-domed mausoleum is eight sided, with twenty-four arches, a big hall, and a verandah. Mughal architecture is largely about symmetry, order, logic, balance, and mathematical symbolism, whereas Hindu architecture is inclined toward the ornamental and adheres to the idea of shotgun housing, where you add on as necessary. The transplendent Taj is set in a formal Persian garden on the bank of the Yamuna River, which gives an added feeling of serenity and harmony.

The Taj is one of those places where you're going to be bombarded by guides and souvenir sellers. All Indian guides firmly believe that they were put on earth to *help*. Oddly enough, "I am guide" repeated dozens of times starts to sound a lot like "I am God." If your tour doesn't come with a guide, then there's a good chance you will want to hire someone to explain the meaning of the Taj's spectacular inlaid jewels, calligraphy, and elaborate design motifs. I didn't like that a lot of children were selling postcards and trinkets, because I worry that the income prohibits their families from sending them to school. But they insisted they were in school, and a spot multiplication and spelling test proved that the ones I quizzed were indeed getting an education and functioning at or above grade level.

Every once in a while, especially during the monsoon rains, the Taj Mahal springs a leak, which romantics describe as the world's most passion-filled monument shedding a tear and engineers describe as a leak. These are swiftly repaired by highly trained professionals using equal parts loving care and mortar.

Many people insist that this shrine to love must be viewed at sunrise or sunset in order to get the full effect, but I can assure you that it looks perfectly majestic at midday. However, there are plenty of hotels in and around Agra if this is on your agenda. If not, it's possible to download photo images of the Taj at all different times of day and install them as your computer wallpaper.

Another reason to be in Agra at sunrise and sunset is to watch the *kabootar baz* (pigeon flyers) in and around the city sending their birds out on maneuvers. This is an ancient sport that was patronized by Mughals and currently culminates in a week-long contest every year in which around ten thousand pigeons are released with the object of getting birds from one team to defect to another team. If nothing else, you'll learn that pigeons traveling together are not called a flock but a kit or a loft.

In addition to the Taj Mahal, you may want to see the double-walled city known as Agra Fort, with its glowing red sandstone, sky-high minarets, and intricate design work. This was refurbished by Mughal emperor Akbar the Great (1542–1605), Shāh Jāhan's grandfather, and used as a base to govern the country. A quick right turn between the outer and inner gates makes the fort safe from elephant attack, since they need a long runway to build up speed, suggesting that the detail-oriented Akbar really did think of everything.

Also nearby is the extravagant red sandstone city of Fatehpur Sikri, India's version of a Colorado ghost town, with eager guides instead of old prospectors. Akbar started construction in 1570, after a Sufi saint foretold the birth of a boy to the as yet sonless emperor, and a little emperor quickly followed (and not long after that, two spares to the heir). This UNESCO World Heritage Site is a distinctive combination of Persian, Indian, and Islamic architecture, although it lasted only fourteen years as the new Mughal royal court. The city was permanently abandoned due to an insufficient water supply. And in keeping with the unsustainability tradition, there still aren't any decent restaurants or watering holes in the area, so brown-bag it or plan to go elsewhere to eat.

Located in Sikandra, a suburb just seven miles northwest of Agra, is Akbar's tomb complex, which is another architectural masterpiece, built with deep red sandstone and white marble so that it aligns with the points on a compass. However, if you're weary of seeing marble and red sandstone tombs and palaces, you can head to the nearby Agra Bear Rescue Facility. Ten years ago on the road from Agra to Fatehpur Sikri, you would've seen dancing bears among the street peddlers and performers. These sloth bears have short hind legs, long nails, and a long, pointy snout to dig up insects, their main source of food. The bears are captured as cubs, which usually means slaughtering the mother bear, and illegally sold to members of the Kalandar tribe, who've been making their living off dancing bears for centuries. The new owner puts a painful, thick metal ring through a sensitive part of the nose using a hot poker and yanks out the bear's canine teeth without anesthetic. Once these operations are completed, the bears are put on very short leashes and forced to perform for the rest of their useful lives. But animal rights activists continued to mount complaints and the practice was finally outlawed in 1972, although this didn't entirely put a stop to it.

More recently, the government decided that because people count on the bears for their livelihood, fifty thousand rupees would be given in exchange for turning in your bear and signing an agreement to get out of the dancing sloth bear business altogether—the Indian equivalent of double secret probation. This is enough money for a Kalandar family to start a small business and give their children an education. As a result, more than a thousand bears are off the streets, and only about sixty remain in remote villages that are difficult to reach, since most don't have roads.

At the Agra Bear Rescue Facility, which is part of the Soor Sarovar Bird Sanctuary, you can see more than 150 species of resident and migratory birds, the aforementioned sloth bears, snakes, some free-ranging antelope, and one camel keeping his head down, trying to blend in with the antelope. The rescued sloth bears cannot be released into the wild and will live out their days here with plenty of room to relax and play, no longer on the end of a four-foot chain, being forced to perform. Still, muscle memory is a powerful thing, and you can catch a number of them going through their old dance routines, but at least they're dancing for themselves.

Now that the dancing bear captors have mostly been put out of business, the sloth bear is under siege by poachers. There's a large market in China for their internal organs, particularly gall bladders, which are used to make natural medicines. Honestly, those sloth bears must be thinking, *If it's not one thing, it's another with you people.*

Safaris, Spas, and Shopping

A good destination after Delhi or Agra is the sand-stone city of Jaipur, capital of the desert state Rajasthan. Delhi, Agra, and Jaipur are known as the Golden Triangle and many tour operators put together packages that include these three famous cities. (Not to be confused with the opium-producing area that includes parts of Myanmar, Vietnam, Laos, and Thailand; the Golden Triangle of rapid economic development that encompasses Shanghai and China; or the Golden Triangle garage band, which cites its influences as crawfish and trash cans and has bestowed upon us such underground favorites as "Cold Bones" and "Neon Noose.") Jaipur is easily accessible from the capital in four to five hours by car, bus, or train, or forty-five minutes by plane. Jaipur is camel country, and if you drive, camels standing by the side of the road are as common a sight as jaywalking cows on the way from Delhi to Agra, pigeons in Central Park, and dog poop on the boulevards of Paris. In 1876, Jaipur painted itself pastel pink (the color of hospitality) to welcome Prince Albert and Queen Elizabeth II, and thus earned the name the Pink City.

There's a wonderful mix of monuments, hilltop forts, preserved palaces, lakes, well-tended gardens, and shopping, which ranges from haggling your way through crowded bazaars to being served tea in fancy, air-conditioned shops. The area is known as a mecca for buying jewelry, blue glaze pottery, crisp organdy linens, and camelskin shoes. A visitor can't help but wonder why the city doesn't put a few more dollars into sprucing up the attractions while addressing the killer pollution and maddening traffic congestion, like other Indian cities that are attracting foreign investment, rapidly expanding, and providing a rising standard of living. Yet development continues apace—an international convention center and a world-class golf course are currently under construction. If you build it, I guess they'll come with a nine iron and an oxygen mask.

On the way to Jaipur, it's worth stopping at the Neemrana Fort-Palace hotel, just sixty miles southwest of Delhi. Built in 1464, this is one of India's oldest heritage resorts (modernized palaces) and commands breathtaking views interrupted only by the occasional screech of a peacock. The heritage hotels usually provide a full line of spa facilities and services, including yoga classes and henna painting. (Yoga tourists repeatedly told me that the yoga instruction in India was the best they'd ever had.) While spa workers are friendly and attentive, be warned that your massage therapist will beat the curry out of you unless advised otherwise, even if she looks like someone's great-grandmother. Make that *especially* if she looks like someone's great-grandmother and remembers when the ruling class of English speakers needed to be taken down a peg. Adventurous travelers can enjoy the aerial zipline to soar over the mountains using equipment that operators proudly guarantee was *not* made in India.

As one leaves the heart of Delhi and heads out through the suburbs, the roads rapidly fill with cows, pigs, dogs, and monkeys. Having once worked on a farm and thus familiar with the fact that a bovine can easily devour a hundred pounds of feed per day, I couldn't help but ask, What do all these cows eat? Free-roaming cows consume lots of bananas, since they grow locally and are therefore cheap and plentiful. Who knew? That fourth stomach is apparently for making fruit smoothies. Otherwise, locals give many of the cows wheat, rice, and vegetables in exchange for their milk. Cows are smarter than one might think and return to the place they're being fed, no matter where they may wander to scavenge during the day. (Water buffalo, on the other hand, are not nearly so bright and must be fetched.) Some temples have food-for-milk relationships with cows that appear to be surviving independently along the roadside. However, when a cow can no longer produce milk, it's usually abandoned to street life, despite its sacred status. A few people, and in some places the local governments, have set up sanctuaries for old, infirm, and cast-off cows.

By day, most cows graze along the roadside, but they obviously think median grass tastes best, so they stand with their two front legs on the median and the majority of their bulk jutting out into a busy street, lined up like they're at a cow lunch counter, and in so doing create a major traffic hazard. Cows have formidable powers of relaxation and can comfortably sprawl in the middle of a highway for hours. Or a cow will stand stock-still in one place in the road for a very long time, as if auditioning to be lawn statuary, thereby lulling drivers into a false sense of security, and then suddenly bust a bovine move. If India were a human body and the highways were arteries taking oxygenated blood away from the heart, then cows are the enormous fat globules blocking the pathways, causing strokes and infarctions and in general killing people before they can say "Holy cow!"

After the Golden Triangle is checked off your list, there's the option of going all Indiana Jones and venturing into the desert. The Thar Desert, also known as the Great Indian Desert, can be toured by camel, horse, or Jeep, which is a terrific way to see the former princely kingdoms of Jaisalmer, Bikaner, Jodhpur, and Pushkar. However, don't be fooled by the word *desert* since it's a lively place where you can see chinkara (gazelles), blackbuck, Bengal fox, wolves, more than 150 varieties of birds, and (surprise!) carpet sellers. The major advantage of traveling by horse is that they're afraid of snakes (like me), whereas camels appear rather indifferent to king cobras, and Jeeps have no sense of mortal danger whatsoever.

It's also possible to head off to one of India's many jungle resorts for bird-watching and tiger-spotting, either by Jeep or on elephant back. If you have your heart set on seeing a tiger in its natural environment, then the best time to visit is April or May, when the heat drives them out of hiding in search of water. Otherwise, nearby Ranthambore National Park is the second best place for tiger-spotting year-round, with its high density of about three dozen big cats. (Bandhavgarh National Park is considered to be the best and is located in the state of Madhya Pradesh, in central India, an overnight train ride from Delhi or a four-to-five-hour drive northeast from the airport in Jabalpur.) Ranthambore served as the hunting grounds for the maharajas of Jaipur and contains a historic fort built in 994 CE. The park is a favorite of nature lovers and wildlife photographers and is now becoming famous as a wedding destination. For all those workaholics being dragged along, your Blackberrys and iPhones will continue to ring and hum amidst all the magnificent flora and fauna or while you're enjoying a fine meal at the rooftop restaurant with its mood music and fully stocked bar that includes watermelon mojitos and mango martinis.

Amer Fort, just outside of Jaipur, is a good spot to take a short ride on a Technicolor elephant, complete with painted toenails. If you're feeling particularly athletic, sign up for a round of elephant polo. Just make sure that you're able to wield an eight-foot-long cane pole with a mallet at the end while riding a three-ton pachyderm.

If you're truly in search of the unusual, along with a great story for the grandkids, the Indian equivalent to our funhouse must be the dazzling white marble Karni Mata Temple, located northwest of Jaipur in the village of Deshnok. As the story goes, the Hindu goddess Karni Mata beseeched Yama, the god of death, to save the dying son of a storyteller, and when Yama refused, she reincarnated all storytellers as rats. The temple is now home to more than twenty thousand rats, and it's considered good luck if the rats scamper across your feet. It's also considered fortunate to eat or drink directly after a rat, from the same spot, but I'd steer clear of that practice, as rats have been known to carry plagues that can kill a hundred million or so people.

The supreme blessing is to spot a white rat, because worshippers believe they're the reincarnation of the goddess Karni Mata and her kin. However, white rats are scarce, and every time one appears the tourist paparazzi race toward it with cameras clicking and lights flashing, so the rat quickly flees back into its hole, which may be why they're scarce in the first place. It's considered bad luck to scamper across a rat, and if you flatten one, then you might be asked to pay restitution, because dead rats are supposed to be replaced with ones of silver or gold. So tread lightly. By the way, this is a Hindu temple, and so you will be removing your shoes before entering. (But socks are okay.)

And now a word about Hindu temples in general. You may suddenly think you're seeing swastikas and wonder if last night's chicken vindaloo was too spicy or if you overdid it on the plum wine. It turns out that the Nazis co-opted the symbol from Sanskrit, where it's the character for the sacred meditative *om*. So don't be alarmed, unless of course you hear the sound of jackboots goose-stepping and the first few bars of "Die Fahne Hoch."

For the extreme sportsperson who is also mechanically minded, there are several auto-rickshaw races that take place around India every year. The Indian Rickshaw Challenge involves traversing the worst roads of the continent while driving and maintaining a pimped-out 1950s three-wheeler. This event is more popularly known as the Amazing Race for the Clinically Insane. Ladies and gentlemen, start your two-stroke engines.

Shall We Gather
at the River?

If you're looking to experience ancient mystical India, then the holy city of Varanasi on the banks of the famous Ganges (aka Ganga) River is the place to go. Located five hundred miles southeast of Delhi, there are daily one-hour flights, or the Shiv Ganga Express train leaves every evening at 6:45 PM and arrives at 7:30 AM the following morning.

Varanasi is also known as "the city of temples," "the religious capital of India," "the city of lights," "the city of learning," and "a holy dump." In his travelogue *Following the Equator*, Mark Twain wrote, "Benares [now Varanasi] is older than history, older than tradition, older even than legend, and looks twice as old as all of them put together." Despite being a sacred place for Hindus and Buddhists, Varanasi's population is almost one-third Muslim, and there's a Saint Mary's Protestant Church and a Roman Catholic infant Jesus shrine just to show that God is indeed everywhere. Or gods, such as the case may be.

A maze of two thousand temples, narrow alleyways, crumbling palaces, rickety staircases, centuries-old sculptures, flower vendors, long-haired holy men, local potentates, loudspeakers belting out prayers, mendicants cradling begging bowls, sandalwood kiosks, and (surprise!) silk shops, the city is truly unlike any other. It takes time to pick your way through all those who are busy hawking, meditating, sleeping, and walking along the winding, uneven streets, and one wouldn't exactly blame nonbelievers for demanding an express lane, since, unlike Hindus, Buddhists, Muslims, and Christians, atheists don't have all eternity. A large number of cows and dogs have managed to weave their way into the fabric of city life, relieving themselves as they go. This, combined with a lack of public lavatories for humans and the aroma of so many burnt offerings, can make one ask, *Who is cooking feet? Because they're done.*

On the bright side, scheming primates don't shake down Varanasi tourists, since people leave plenty of food offerings in the many different temples, and the monkeys help these gifts reach the gods by moving them upward in the universe, starting with nearby tree branches and rooftops.

Guides in Varanasi, following the initial push necessary to secure your business, are helpful and friendly, but just as tours of Istanbul end at a rug shop, all outings here conclude at a textile or glass-bead stall. Shopping tip: a good pashmina scarf should pass through a ring the size that you'd wear on a finger. Your guide will surely inform you that Goldie Hawn has been to Varanasi and ask if you'd like to see a photo of her with a famous guru. This would be the appropriate time to ask if your guide would like to see a YouTube clip of Goldie Hawn on the old sketch comedy show *Laugh-In*.

Unlike the Wailing Wall in Jerusalem, the Holy Mosque in Mecca, or Saint Peter's Basilica in Vatican City, there isn't a specific structure to head for in Varanasi. The *ghats* (stone steps) along the riverbank are the main focal point of Varanasi, as that's where ritual bathing and cremation takes place. To Hindus, the river itself is a deity in that it is believed to have the power to cure ills, expiate sins, and offer a gateway to the next world. More than fifteen hundred miles in length, the Ganges flows down from the Himalayas in an arc across northern India, from west to east, and then runs into the Bay of Bengal. Myths and legends tell various stories of kings, gods, and goddesses who played a role in the divine waters falling from heaven to earth, and even the most nonbelieving of Indians will most likely concede that the Ganges is sacred. Even that old atheist Jawaharlal Nehru, the first prime minister of independent India, wanted a handful of his ashes scattered there. "The Ganga is the river of India, beloved of her people, 'round which are intertwined her racial memories, her hopes and fears, her songs of triumph, her victories and her defeats," he wrote in his will. "She has been a symbol of India's age-long culture and civilization, ever-changing, ever-flowing, and yet ever the same Ganga."

The must-get in Varanasi for your blog or Facebook page is to take one of the many inexpensive boats for hire (complete with operator) out on the river at sunrise or sunset, where hundreds of candles and flower garlands are launched as offerings to Ganga, who is thought to be a living goddess in Hinduism, while temple bells chime and prayers are chanted.

As a result, Varanasi is the perfect town for morning people, and things start rolling at around 3:00 AM. So if you're an insomniac, have jet lag, or just drank too much espresso last night, you can begin sightseeing and souvenir hunting almost immediately. By dawn, the riverbank is chockablock with pilgrims intensely involved in al fresco meditation, salvation seeking, purification, cremation, and a substantial amount of clothes washing.

At first one assumes that it must be the poor and outcast who are burned outdoors for all to see, with dogs and cows meandering past, and then have their remains dumped into the nearby river. In reality, this sacred ceremony is the dream of every Hindu, since it ensures that all sin is washed away and that they'll receive enlightenment in the next life. Despite white cloth coverings, it's possible to make out the various body parts, so unlike saying good-bye at most funerals, watching corpses as they slowly burn is extremely real, or vérité if you happen to be holding a video camera. Apparently some cremations take longer than others, and I witnessed a young man waiting for a friend or relative to finish burning while chatting away on his cell phone. Indeed, life goes on. Same with death. As soon as one body is finished, a new fire is lit, and the next corpse is pulled into place.

India, in general, and Varanasi, in particular, is famous for being a place where spiritual tourists can catch hold of the meaning of existence. Watching so many bodies being cremated along the riverbank, I was reminded of what novelist Franz Kafka said: "Life has meaning because it ends." And though most people don't have control over when they die, for folks living in my heavily Catholic hometown of blizzard-prone Buffalo, this usually means trying to wait until spring so the ground has thawed. Their city having been voted the nation's friendliest by USA Today, Buffalonians prefer not to be a burden to anyone in life or death.

Is it safe for the adventurous Westerner to swim in the Ganges? No, it is not. Honestly, aside from the many cows that love to go skinny-dipping in the Ganges, *nobody* should be in the river in its current polluted state, which features industrial chemicals, partially cremated bodies, and untreated sewage that can quickly result in hepatitis, cholera, dysentery, and other serious maladies. But the locals seem to have a much higher tolerance for their own environment, along with the proper immunities, much like I was able to frolic in contaminated Lake Erie during the 1970s while a Varanasi Hindu might have instantly sunk to the bottom. In July 2010, a twenty-year-old British tourist swam in the Ganges and died several days later, ill with diarrhea. The amount of fecal coliform bacteria alone is way above what the surgeon general recommends for bathing.

To help clean up the water, a special breed of scavenger turtle that feasts on wayward rotting flesh was introduced into the Ganges during the 1990s. Things looked promising at the beginning, as people arrived at the shore with dead bodies in bags, and marauding gangs of tissue-hungry turtles charged ashore and attempted to haul away the corpses. But these primordial beasts turned out to be no match for the mighty river and soon disappeared from sight, presumed to have become corpses themselves. However, you can still find the piranhas, crocodiles, and bull sharks that have been known to attack bathers in the Ganges. Otherwise, the current is strong, and many people drown. If you feel the need for a ritual, then dip your hand in the water and sprinkle some on your head, or better yet, light a candle and set it afloat.

On the positive side, there's a plan in place to

bring the Ganges back from the dead. The Indian government recently committed $4 billion for the purpose of cleaning up the river, which includes prohibiting industrial effluents and providing backup power for enough sewage-treatment plants to meet Varanasi's estimated needs through 2030. The government is also financing a pilot project for a series of treatment ponds that use bacteria to digest waste and can be run with minimal power.

Easy side trips from Varanasi are to the city Sarnath, where Buddha gave his first sermon, and Allahabad, where the Hindu god Brahma is supposed to have made his first sacrifice after creating the world. Allahabad is the meeting place of India's two holiest rivers, the Ganges and the Yamuna, and also, according to Hindu legend, the ancient Sarasvati, which supposedly dried up in the Thar Desert. Allahabad is also one of the four sites where, every twelve years, the Purna Kumbh Mela festival attracts millions of people for some ritual bathing and is usually good for a *CBS News Sunday Morning* segment. Wandering among the many seekers, tourists, and TV producers are naked spiritual men known as *naga sadhus*. (It's not such a shock to see a colorfully painted, long-haired naked man standing in the midst of a large group of revelers so much as it is to see a naked man talking on a cell phone—where does *that* get stored?) In 2001, more than 60 million people showed up, making it the world's largest human gathering in recorded history. The next Purna Kumbh Mela is in 2013. Obviously, these celebrations are not for the claustrophobic pilgrim. Furthermore, if you were raised by a hygiene-crusading nurse convinced that every highway rest stop was a breeding ground for flesh-eating bacteria, as I was, you are wondering how millions of people go to the bathroom in a place where toilets are in short supply to begin with. About eighty thousand corrugated tin squat-holes are set up around the grounds, but if you recall simple division from elementary school, the odds of using one aren't great, so think camping.

My last night in Varanasi, slightly curried out and ready to mix things up a bit, I stumbled upon the only Chinese restaurant in town. After some American-style chow mein, I enjoyed the hot, sweet, syrup-covered Indian dessert known as *lavang latika*, which is similar to Greek baklava or a Mexican sopapilla with pistachio nuts. While sipping a woodsy, earthy oolong tea, I read the message in my fortune cookie, "First find out who everybody else is. You are what is left over." To discover the meaning of life, I'd had to go to the exact spot where East meets East.

Oh! Kolkata!

Calcutta, now known as Kolkata, lies 430 miles to the southeast of Varanasi and is the capital of the state of West Bengal. Like Buffalo, New York, which got a bad rap for blizzards, Rust Belt remorse, and the blue-collar blues, Calcutta became famous for human blight after the huge migrations that followed Partition in 1947 and the Indo-Pakistani War of 1971. Adding insult to injury, Mother Teresa's good works seemed only to enhance its image as a hellhole.

What about the Black Hole of Calcutta? Calcutta was established by the East India Company (a joint-stock venture formed by the British) in 1690 to serve as a trading post. In 1756, the British settlement at Calcutta was overrun by the army of the Muslim ruler Siráj-ud-Dawlah, also called the nabob of Bengal. Angered by the muckety-muck airs and independent attitude of the English-speaking community, Siráj-ud-Dawlah ransacked and destroyed the outpost. At Fort William, a group of British captives were imprisoned in an airless guard room measuring fourteen by eighteen feet—the Black Hole of Calcutta. Some reports say that as many as 146 British were made captive, of whom only twenty-three survived until the next day. Others say that only sixty-four people were held, and twenty-one lived to tell the tale. Modern historians question whether the atrocity happened at all and theorize that it was used as propaganda against Sirāj-ud-Dawlah to demonstrate the barbarity of the natives. Either way, the following year the British recaptured the city, expanded their sphere of influence, and decided to rule India as a colony.

Calcutta was the capital of all India (and what is today Pakistan and Bangladesh) until 1911, when the British transferred the government to New Delhi, much the way ours was moved from Manhattan to Washington, DC, after a pit stop in Philly. But, like New York City, Calcutta has always been the arts and intellectual capital of the country, and, like New York, it will be a fantastic city once they finally finish it. Calcutta is home to more literary magazines, movie houses, concert halls, and theater companies than any other metropolis in Asia. Poetry readings regularly attract hundreds of listeners. (Meantime, American poet Thomas Lynch says that he considers a successful event one where poetry readers don't outnumber audience members.) And cinemas have Full House signs from afternoon until evening (although young people use movies as intimacy opportunities).

The city has been home to India's three Nobel

laureates, including the famous Bengali poet Rabindranath Tagore. It was Tagore who gave Mohandas Gandhi the honorific *Mahatma*, meaning "great soul." Although Tagore was later dismayed when Gandhi claimed the great earthquake that rocked Bihar in 1934 and killed at least seven thousand people was punishment for discrimination against untouchables. (Other accounts put the death toll upward of thirty thousand, but most Indian disasters seem to have a footnote after the death toll saying "plus or minus twenty-five thousand," the same way that Western pharmaceutical companies add three pages of fine print warning that there's a good chance their drugs will kill you.) The prophetlike Tagore was a playwright, philosopher, poet, actor, author, artist, musician, educational reformer, and women's libber who is infinitely quotable, but some standouts include "The butterfly counts not months but moments, and has time enough," "Don't limit a child to your own learning, for he was born in another time," and "The highest education is that which does not merely give us information but makes our life in harmony with all existence." Still left with time on his hands, Tagore penned the Indian national anthem "Jana-Gana-Mana" *and* the Bangladeshi national anthem "Amar Shonar Bangla." Talk about an overachiever. In Los Angeles, it's considered multitasking to be a singing waiter with a screenplay in your back pocket.

There's Western philosophy and Eastern philosophy, Western medicine and Eastern medicine, and
while there's Western dentistry, Eastern dentistry still
appears to be a question mark, based on the look of
some of the street stalls offering low-cost oral treat-
ments. No one is asking you to bite down on a bullet
or swig whiskey, but let's just say that between patients
I didn't see any hand washing, and Shiva only knows
what that large flathead screwdriver is for.

Bengalis are food aficionados who take great
pride in their native cuisine, which is famous for its
mixture of subtle and fiery flavors. The big dish to try
out is *macher jhol*, a fish curry spiced with mustard,
which literally translates as "fish in gravy" and can be
prepared without the fish for vegetarians. The region is
also famous for its desserts, mostly made of sweetened
and finely ground cottage cheese. The names in and of
themselves are mouthwatering—*shondesh, roshogolla,
laddu, pantua,* and *chomchom.* Cakes, yogurts, and
custards are likewise popular treats.

On the must-see list is the Calcutta flower market, with its glorious profusion of color and activity.
Flowers are an enormous part of Indian culture and
are used every day for festivals, weddings, funerals, and
entertaining. Workers dash pell-mell while balancing
enormous piles of garlands on their heads, and vendors hawk their vibrant wares from booths and mats
on the ground as overloaded bullock carts push their

way through what appears to be mass floral confusion. As a tourist, you aren't the intended buyer for these wholesalers and will find yourself largely left in peace to enjoy the sight of bright orange and yellow marigolds, cape lilies, hibiscus, white freesia, long-stem red roses, blue barleria, and wild water plum, so long as you watch where you're going or else risk being run over by a donkey in the name of capitalism.

The flower market is located next to the stately eight-lane Howrah Bridge, one of the largest cantilevered structures in the world. This landmark bridge across the Hugli River is currently under siege by, of all things, spit. Having weathered monsoons, survived being struck by a barge, and endured the wear and tear of the sixty thousand vehicles and fifty thousand pedestrians that cross each day, the key struts that support the bridge's girders are corroding from saliva.

Roadside stands that appear to be selling hundreds of varieties of individually wrapped condoms are actually trading in packs of *paan* (betel leaf with areca nut and slaked lime mixed with various flavors), a mild stimulant similar to our chewing tobacco. The result is that a large number of men with permanently stained teeth continuously spew millions of mouthfuls of paan in all directions. Almost every wall and sidewalk in Calcutta is covered with telltale vivid red splotches that make it look as if Elmer Fudd went on a varmint-shooting rampage. Studies have been designed to assess spit damage to public structures, and if the Howrah Bridge continues to collect loogies at the current rate, it will soon have to be closed for repairs.

Crackdowns on paan-spitting are under way all across the country. In Mumbai, commuters caught expectorating on trains might be surrounded by spit activists armed with mops, pails, and bad attitudes who force offenders to join bucket brigades. In Delhi, where large amounts of public funds are spent on scrubbing paan stains from walls and pavement, authorities have started a public awareness campaign to drive down the practice and thrown public urination into the mix, which is also playing a role in corroding buildings and landmarks. If you opt for total immersion and decide to experiment with paan, be careful that you don't break a tooth on the woody betel nut and end up in an open-air dentist's chair on a Calcutta side street at midnight.

Bidis are small, foul-smelling hand-rolled Indian cigarettes made with cheap tobacco and smoked by more than 100 million people, mostly the poor and illiterate, resulting in at least two hundred thousand tuberculosis deaths per year. The most popular form of tobacco product in India, bidis also cause lung cancer and mouth cancer along with heart and lung disease. Children, especially tribal and street children, often start smoking these highly addictive cigarettes as early as age eight. Workers who roll bidis and the farmers who handle the tobacco crop also suffer from severe health problems.

Another top Calcutta sightseeing stop is the white marble Victoria Memorial Hall, complete with museum, art gallery, and well-tended park—the British response to the Taj Mahal. It was built to commemorate Queen Victoria's 1901 diamond jubilee, celebrating sixty years on the throne, though the Empress of India never deigned to visit the jewel in her crown. Locals obviously have mixed feelings about a shrine to a former colonial ruler who was occasionally given *actual Indian people* as gifts, but they allow it, as the monument is attractive and good for tourism.

India is replete with complexities and contradictions, and Mother Teresa is one of those. She helped thousands of Calcutta's destitute, orphaned, helpless, sick, and dying through her Order of the Missionaries of Charity and is currently shortlisted by the Vatican for sainthood. It's possible to visit the Calcutta Motherhouse, the room where Mother Teresa worked and slept, and also her tomb. For anyone wanting to serve as a short-term volunteer, there are no preliminary requirements—just attend one of the briefings given three times a week. It's not necessary to be Catholic, and most participants find the experience to be exceptionally gratifying.

As Mother Teresa expanded her organization around the globe, questions were raised about accepting funds from third world dictators and Mafia dons, the use of donations, and also the condition of her facilities.

With regard to the standard of care, if you were at the Calcutta location, it was because you had nowhere else to go, as Mother Teresa's order specifically served "the poorest of the poor," and the alternative was dying alone in the streets, the fate of many, so complaining about the cleanliness of the towels and lack of morphine is somewhat counterintuitive, in my opinion. Critics also wondered why, when Mother Teresa experienced heart problems and age-related illnesses, she sought treatment at an upscale hospital in California and other high-end clinics. Otherwise, her position against contraception was very much at odds with India's population crisis in the latter half of the twentieth century.

Not far away is the Kali Temple, Hinduism's holiest pilgrimage center in Calcutta, which is dedicated to the multitalented goddess associated with time, change, destruction, liberation, and eternal energy. It features a vibrant botanical-and-peacock decoration scheme, complete with rainbow highlights that make an Italian living room look plain by comparison and an image of the goddess Kali with a long, protruding tongue fashioned out of gold. Beware of wandering priests who attempt to move you toward the donation altar. And know that they've probably cooked the books so that the ledger of contributions most certainly lists fake entries of one thousand rupees (about twenty-five dollars) and higher. With my fair hair and skin (sunbathing for a Pedersen is akin to putting a silver serving spoon in the microwave), I was a standout for being ushered to the front of long lines, given blessings, offered special tours, and asked to donate accordingly. My advice, especially if you're a vegetarian, would be to get out before the ritual goat beheading. On the plus side, over the past few centuries, they've substituted goats for humans.

As the third largest city in a newly industrialized developing country, Calcutta faces the socioeconomic challenges one might expect. A legal red-light district, known as Sonagachi, is home to hundreds of multistory brothels and more than ten thousand sex workers. The Durbar Mahila Samanwaya Committee operates the Sonagachi Project, along with several others in the state, to legalize prostitution, protect sex workers from harassment, provide medical attention for the women and their children, run literacy and vocational programs, and offer financial counseling. Still, the existence of the area is controversial. While certain local, national, and international organizations want all prostitution legalized and regulated, others want it completely outlawed. Some observers insist that claims by Sonagachi's administrators to have drastically reduced the rate of HIV and their intolerance of prostitution by minors or those who've been sold into slavery are overblown.

Unfortunately, Calcutta is known as a hub for traffickers who sell girls as young as ten from Nepal, Bangladesh, and Myanmar into its brothels. Many are then resold to work in Mumbai, the Middle East, and Africa. It's estimated that 1.8 million children per year enter the commercial sex trade. As a matter of interest, the Oscar-winning documentary *Born Into Brothels: Calcutta's Red Light Kids* follows the lives of children born to prostitutes in Sonagachi, while *Half the Sky: Turning Oppression into Opportunity for Women Worldwide*, the acclaimed book by Nicholas D. Kristof and Sheryl WuDunn, has been made into a TV special for the PBS series *Independent Lens*.

Calcutta is known for having strong unions (including one for sex workers) and therefore *bandhs* (strikes) occur regularly, shuttering stores and halting all transportation, including trains and taxis. However, citizens are tiring of these demonstrations of power by local politicians, which end up costing citizens their earnings and cause countless aggravations to an already difficult daily life. And tourists forced to rent cars aren't exactly thrilled either. Recall that in India they drive on the left while the steering wheel is on the right and the cows are in the middle.

Calcutta is still plagued by the heartrending poverty and dire living conditions that result from an oversubscribed and thereby inadequate government safety net. Leprosy, a disease that has been eradicated in most parts of the world, continues to run rampant here, and you can see its victims begging along the roadside, propelling themselves atop jerry-built skids.

The government does offer medical attention and a place to live for lepers, but the rules they must follow are strict, and many opt out the way some people in the United States prefer street life over city-run shelters and hospitalization.

In this metropolis of 20 million, which is larger than Los Angeles and San Francisco combined, almost two-thirds of the residents survive in teeming slums or overcrowded streets. Thousands of children work from dawn until dusk, seven days a week, as pickers, climbing through piles of rubbish in search of anything saleable. Unfortunately, this is a fact of life in all Indian cities, but it's most prevalent here in the poverty-stricken northeast. Street children are usually malnourished and experience high rates of cancer from exposure to hazardous materials. In effect, they are society's refuse.

There are laws about compulsory schooling, but they lack enforcement. Private charities, such as the Hope Kolkata Foundation and the Akshar Gyan Charitable Trust, in Mumbai, are dedicated to getting slum children education, healthcare, and employment. The Unitarian Universalist Holdeen India Program works to secure human rights along with social and economic justice for those marginalized on the basis of gender, caste, ethnicity, religion, or sexual orientation. Otherwise, government programs operate so that the poor can receive staple items such as milk and wheat, but a corrupt and inefficient bureaucracy often prevents them from receiving their rations. Recent estimates cite two-thirds of government grain allotments as being stolen or contaminated.

Bureaucracy is the biggest legacy left by the British, goes the joke in India, where bribes, kickbacks, reams of red tape, and incompetence on a massive scale are part of daily life. Each year, more than 2 million people take the exam for about eighty entry-level Indian Administrative Service positions. It is said that if you are accepted, your family will have enough to eat for seven generations. However, it's rumored that to even get the job in the first place, a bribe is required.

As a result, bribery has become a way of life. For instance, if you build a house and want water, it's necessary to see a local revenue officer for land details, go to another office for verification, submit an application for a water connection, wait for approval, take the approval to the lower court, get an affidavit that you won't be using the water for agricultural purposes, submit all the documents, await verification, petition the water authority, and make an appointment for installation. This process takes from six months to a year and costs from two hundred to four hundred dollars. Alternatively, you could get the affidavit that you won't be farming and pay a bribe of about five hundred dollars to a water authority officer, and in two hours you'll be happily taking a hot shower while a pot of mulligatawny soup simmers in the kitchen.

Many police officers are not there to protect citizens, but for the purpose of extortion. If you're in a car accident, there's oftentimes a bidding war in which both sides attempt to coerce the police to report their version of events. The officers may even go to your home a few days after the accident to continue the shakedown. Meantime, truckers trying to go from one Indian state to another might as well be attempting to cross into another country. Checkpoints are so numerous, slow, and rife with payoffs that several days' time and about 30 percent in corruption costs must be added to the transport schedule. Perhaps this is why almost all truckers from India and Pakistan turn out to be frustrated abstract expressionists operating vehicles decorated with flamboyant colors, psychedelic patterns, and a profusion of bling, with no inch remaining unadorned. Jackson Pollock would have been right at home with a paintbrush in one hand and a cigarette in the other on the Grand Trunk Road.

It transpires that the most popular Indian curry of all is to curry favor with a well-placed bribe. One story has a South Mumbai restaurateur listing a large expenditure under the heading Dog Food. The income tax officer wouldn't pass the accounts without questioning the entrepreneur, who explained, "It's for the two-legged dogs from your department who come begging and whom I need to pay off every once in a while." The accounts were then approved. Still, this anecdote isn't much different than the many I've heard over the years about building, bridge, and health inspectors being bribed in New York.

It can be enormously difficult to obtain documents such as a passport or birth certificate. An American woman working for the State Department in India said, "In the United States, when you go to the Department of Motor Vehicles for your license you expect to come out with your license. Not here. Not unless your uncle knows somebody." Imagine putting the DMV forward as an example of the best America has to offer when it comes to service with a smile!

The closest I came to a scam was in Calcutta, when a thirtysomething man with slicked-back hair and wearing a worn white suit walked over and complimented me on my necklace. I was immediately suspicious, because the beaded necklace was inexpensive and far from what would be considered good jewelry. It transpired that his uncle was a highly talented jewelry manufacturer, but the government had prohibitively high export fees and taxes, so he couldn't sell his goods overseas. If I were willing to take some items home with me (he didn't inquire where home was) and hand them off to another party, then I'd get a healthy cut of the profits upon delivery. I immediately assumed that drugs were involved and envisioned a German shepherd alerting customs agents to my hash stash, followed by a life sentence in a Thai prison with a sadistic warden and no HBO. However, the con here is to give the traveler a bag of worthless glass stones or paste jewelry in exchange for putting up some security, such as money or a real gold watch, and no one ever meets you at your destination. But I was much too clever to fall for that, and besides, I'm about to reap rich rewards by helping a wealthy Nigerian government official with an embarrassing legal problem to transfer millions of dollars, out of which I'll be entitled to keep a *very* large percentage of the total.

Salaam Mumbai!

In 1985, a catchy song called "We Built This City" (on rock and roll) was recorded by the group Starship (part of Jefferson Airplane and Jefferson Starship after a lawsuit) and made its way to number one on the US *Billboard* Hot 100. The lyrics included the Golden Gate Bridge and The City by the Bay, both references to San Francisco, a metropolis I was under the impression had been built on the Gold Rush of 1849 rather than rock and roll. Meantime, lead female vocalist Grace Slick said the song was actually written about early 1970s Los Angeles, which I was under the impression had been built largely on the movie industry. So I'm thinking of writing a pop song called "Ain't Manhattan Grande" describing how New York City was developed atop the world's largest coffee bean. It will explain the ways in which caffeine has leached into the water table, causing millions of hyperactive residents to pinwheel from subway to pharmacy among teams of java speculators trying to buy up all the fountains. Central Park may actually be the lid on the world's largest espresso.

Nevertheless, I can tell you with a degree of certainty that the city of Bombay was built on opium. (I can also tell you with assurance that Mumbai was known as Bombay until 1996, when many Indian cities were shedding their colonial names for something more Indian. However, most people still call it Bombay.) Starting around 1800, Bombay went from being a minor British outpost to the leading exporter of opium and raw cotton, mostly to China. The East India Company had local peasants grow opium, which was then smuggled to China and sold in return for tea and silk, while the profits went back to England. (The only problem with this triangle was that it depended on the Chinese being addicted to opium for it to work.) In fact, Sir Jamsetjee Jejeebhoy, the first Indian to be knighted (1842) and win a baronetcy (1857), was part of the world's largest opium trading network, one of the six directors of the Bank of Bombay, and currently has a famous art school and a hospital named after him. The capital accumulated during this time period successfully laid the groundwork for the modern and industrial port city we now call Mumbai.

So, because of its drug cartel history, you don't see any historic monuments, forts, palaces, temples, or mosques from the distant past around the immense metropolis that is now Mumbai. Furthermore, a large statue of an opium poppy might not convey the desired effect. This island city was and is all about commerce.

That said, Mumbai has a spiritual side, like all of India, and is home to the Hindu holy sect called the Standing Babas, also known as Khareshwari. These men, usually former military, police, or civil servants, take a vow to never sit or lie down again (or at least for twelve years) in order to burn off bad karma through physical deprivation and gain spiritual enlightenment. They eat, work, pray, and go to the toilet standing up and use a swing to keep from toppling over while asleep. This is a painful lifestyle choice that causes their legs and feet to permanently swell and develop ulcers. I didn't see any Standing Babas during my stay in Mumbai, but other tourists reported spotting them at the Kumbh Mela festival in Varanasi, and it's possible to view some arresting photos on the Internet of men with painted faces and wild hair who appear to be one lab accident away from becoming comic book super-villains. So next time you're stuck waiting in a long line, hanging onto a pole in a subway car, or standing over the sink washing the Thanksgiving dishes, imagine what it'd be like to never sit down again. That said, Standing Baba does not appear to be an occupation currently open to women and children—but don't get me wrong, I'm not lodging a complaint.

Today, Mumbai is the financial and entertainment capital of India, home to the stock exchange and Bollywood, and the richest and most populous city in India. In fact, it was just added to the list of the world's wealthiest cities, albeit one distinctly lacking a metro system. On the bright side, Mumbai has enclosed bus shelters with seats for its many tired commuters. Wake up, NYC.

Even more than New York and Los Angeles, Mumbai is a twenty-four-hour city, its streets packed at midnight with people out shopping, eating, and getting haircuts. The city is so cosmopolitan that not only are there no longer cows in the roads, but they've done away with human-pulled and human-pedaled rickshaws. It's officially the automobile age on the highways and byways of Mumbai, which has unfortunately resulted in a cloud of pollution that sits atop the city and refuses to blow out to sea. There's also a tremendous amount of traffic congestion, and rush hour is basically all the time. However, this cuts way down on accidents, since it's hard to move fast enough to have anything other than a fender bender, even if you're texting at the wheel.

The seven islands that make up Mumbai are a wild hodgepodge of gleaming new glass and granite office towers, floodlit fountains, construction sites, open latrines, neon lights, potholed roads, highways in the making, crumbling relics of the British Empire, sagging storefronts, food stalls, and apartment buildings in various stages of rising up and falling down. The air is filled with traffic noise, diesel fuel, unfiltered exhaust, cooking smells, and strands of music. Dotting the horizon are lights from hundreds of ships anchored along the coastline and the gigantic flames that leap from the towers of offshore oil rigs.

In November 2008, a series of ten coordinated shootings and bombings across the city killed at least 173 people and wounded more than 308. Behind the commando-style terrorist attacks was the Pakistani militant group Lashkar-e-Taiba, whose goal is to make South Asia into an Islamic theocracy and free the Muslims in Kashmir who are living under Indian governance. Such incidents make it easy to understand India's current love/hate relationship with us, since we send billions of American tax dollars to Pakistan that are supposed be used to fight the Taliban, but more often than not this exercise ends the same way as sending a teenager to the grocery store with a credit card and expecting them to make healthy choices.

Although usually referred to as Kashmir, the northwest state of Jammu and Kashmir consists of two major parts—Jammu, which is predominantly Hindu, and the valley of Kashmir, which is mostly Muslim. A third part, Ladakh, is largely Buddhist. Kashmir shares a boundary with both India and Pakistan, so following Partition, this predominantly Muslim area with a Hindu maharaja, after some unpleasant noise by Pakistani guerrillas, opted to go with India. This has resulted in an ongoing dispute between India and Pakistan, which erupted into two full-out wars, in 1965 and 1999. Nowadays, various areas are controlled by Pakistan, India, and China, and basically no one is happy. Kashmir is the disputed summer house in a really long, ugly divorce between rich people who both want the place to spite the other. (China appears to favor Pakistan, in addition to its own interests.) The only light at the end of this tunnel is that the locals are getting worn down by fighting, curfews, and not being able to send their children to school. Having grown up in Buffalo, New York, I know how close to a nervous breakdown mothers can get on the fifth snow day in a row, so my bet is on a peace agreement sometime soon.

Still, tourists can visit Kashmir, and authorities insist that the state is relatively safe. It's possible to rent houseboats, buy famed Kashmiri carpets and handicrafts, and see Asia's largest tulip garden in the Zabarwan foothills. In fact, Kashmir recently inaugurated its first five-star hotel, the Taj Vivanta, located on a hilltop overlooking scenic Dal Lake, which also goes by the nickname Srinagar's Jewel. Just try and ignore the fact that the place known as Paradise on Earth has soldiers and security guards armed with automatic weapons stationed pretty much everywhere.

About twenty of India's twenty-eight states are also dealing with a Maoist insurgency called the Naxalite movement. A May 2010 train wreck ninety miles west of Calcutta that killed 115 and injured more than 140 is believed to be the result of their sabotaging the tracks. The rebels, who have somewhere between ten thousand and twenty thousand fighters, according to the Home Ministry, believe in extreme violence and protracted struggle and claim to be fighting on behalf of the rural poor, who have supposedly been left out of the country's economic progress. Others insist that this isn't so much a homegrown Communist party as a Chinese-backed terrorist organization looking to destabilize all of India.

As a result of recent terror attacks, many hotels, shopping malls, cinemas, and points of interest now have metal detectors and bag inspectors. Sadly, it's probably the direction in which we're all headed, and entering T.G.I. Friday's at happy hour will soon require a full body-cavity search. (Is it my imagination, or do these types of chain restaurants have a penchant for naming blender drinks after natural disasters, a strategy they may want to rethink if operating in mudslide-, earthquake-, and tsunami-scarred South Asia?) When I was a kid, people used to brag about how little security they had, and now people brag about how much security they have. We splurged on one of those faux gray rocks that held a house key and cleverly placed it among the pachysandra, fooling no one, since all the neighbors had the same faux gray rock somewhere within a few feet of their front door.

In all large Indian cities, it's possible for tourists to go on slum tours, and there are arguments for and against these that, in my opinion, are about equal, so it's up to the individual. Opponents say that there's a loss of dignity for the slum dwellers, as they perform many of their daily activities in full view of passersby throughout the acres of shacks that are no more than patchworks of rags, plastic, scrap metal, bamboo, and cardboard attached to one another, with narrow lanes winding between them. Advocates of these tours claim that viewing such grim poverty firsthand brings a greater level of awareness or a hot flush of shame and hopefully some help. Perhaps the worst of it is to find out that certain slums have waiting lists to get in! Every day, more people are moving to the cities from their villages, while those on the streets are trying to find shelter, a stove, and a ration of water.

Of course, slums are not an Indian invention. When I first moved to Manhattan in the early 1980s, Tompkins Square Park was a Hooverville and the Bowery not unlike the streets of Calcutta. Meantime, the United States has impoverished areas in all of its cities and rural places such as Appalachia, accompanied by all of the poverty-related social problems. Likewise, there are urban neighborhoods and entire towns that have been devastated by crack cocaine and crystal methamphetamine, while families are without teeth as a result of addiction to sugar-infested soft drinks.

In addition to being the headquarters for many national and international corporations, Mumbai is a showcase for the entrepreneurial spirit of India, much like Bangalore (now officially known as Bengaluru, but no one seems willing to call it that) is considered the Indian Silicon Valley. Call centers in particular have hired thousands of women workers and drastically improved their standard of living. There, Haimavati from Himatnagar is miraculously transformed into Debbie from Duluth, although nowadays call centers are more likely to be phoning us to ask when we expect to make a payment on that big old credit card bill than helping with our airline reservations. And with the way India's economy is growing, Americans may soon be jockeying for jobs as the cabbies who drive them to and from their new office buildings. Or when a cardiologist in New Delhi calls to make a booking on Air India, Bob from Buffalo is going to answer the phone and pretend to be Siddhartha from Sangareddy.

With a fast-growing middle and upper class, the city has become the capital of mom-and-pop cosmetic surgery shops, which often feature underqualified doctors and cheap, uncertified, or reconditioned equipment. With little or no regulation on who can practice, there's little opportunity to sue for mishaps. But people are lined up for all sorts of procedures, since they feel it provides better jobs and marriage prospects. This is thought to be a direct result of overexposure to movies, models, and advertising, which, in addition to a desire for plastic surgery, has likewise led to higher rates of depression. Sound familiar?

Mumbai also serves as a major hub for India's reproductive tourism industry, which brings in more than half a billion dollars a year. Whereas surrogacy can cost $100,000 in the United States, in India it's one-quarter of that, with few questions asked. Almost all applicants are accepted—gay couples, older couples, single parents, and those who just can't find the time. *Made in India* is a recent feature-length documentary that takes an unvarnished look at this as-yet unregulated market.

The multibillion dollar Bollywood industry is said to be run by the Indian Mafia. But in a place where a court case often takes decades to wend its way through the system, where it can take years for a farmer to get a loan, or months to have a landline telephone installed, this is probably a good thing, or else the movies would still be in black-and-white and possibly without sound.

The archetypal Hindi-language Bollywood film is a form of escape, which is why it's a three-and-a-half-hour musical spectacular of romance and violence. Usually a pair of lovers cannot be together due to some obstacle such as parental disapproval or betrothal to another. Best friends can be counted on to have a misunderstanding. The hero is a proud underdog, either a rickshaw driver or a laborer. The lovers fight all odds to be together, which involves the obligatory wet-sari scene, fight scene, sobbing mothers, and a car chase, until they're finally united. Bollywood films are censored, and although the rules seem to be vague and inconsistent, for the most part you won't see tonsil hockey kissing, nudity, or heavy drug use, and in 2005 smoking was banned, but rape scenes and bloodshed appear to be welcome. However, Indian filmmakers have recently been making high-quality films in other genres, including documentary and animation, that are doing well nationally as well as around the globe and being nominated for prestigious industry awards.

A terrific place for respite from the hustle and bustle of Mumbai is the Hanging Gardens. With its splendid flower beds, sculpted topiary, and premier vista overlooking the Arabian Sea, this is the ideal place to watch the sun set. Best of all, there are no metal detectors, no noise, no crime to speak of, no one trying to sell you postcards, and no gangsta monkeys shaking down tourists for food. The famous thugs (marauding murderers) are long gone, and it's even safe for a foreign woman walking on her own. If I received any strange looks, it was because Indians tend to have straight, dark hair while mine is more like an apricot-colored humidity gauge, and when you see it rising there's a low-pressure system moving inland that's usually followed by small craft warnings. Most visitors to the garden are couples strolling together or families having an outing, so there's no unwanted attention from men.

The sexual harassment that occurs on the street is known as Eve teasing, and, unfortunately, it's rather prevalent in some places, particularly around boys' high schools. Government officials insist that they're in the process of making laws against sexual harassment tougher and having public areas policed more vigilantly, but victims claim the legal system currently works against them and in favor of the accused. However, if you're an American woman traveling alone or with a few other women, these roadside Romeos shouldn't be a problem, since Indians love to watch American action movies and will assume you carry a gun, like Angelina Jolie in *Salt*, and are not afraid to use it. This raises the delicate point that Americans don't have a particular "look," and theoretically anyone could be an American. That said, unless you've really gone native, most people can spot an American faster than a finger in their chili. Who knows? Maybe it's the low-riding sweatpants with Juicy across the butt or the sweater with the appliquéd reindeer on the front or the bright green Crocs with yellow lightning Jibbitz.

The other famous evening seaside promenade is Chowpatty Beach, a perfect stop for some local color and the occasional political rally. During the day, it's mostly a place for the slumbering unemployed, but in the evening, there's a carnival atmosphere featuring acrobats, monkey shows, head massages, pony rides, short plays, astrologers, and a Ferris wheel. Fast-food stalls offer cotton candy, corn on the cob, and coconut water, along with local favorites such as crisp puffed rice with vegetables and lentil-flour noodles covered in chutney served with *puri*, a deep-fried flatbread. It's for you to decide whether or not you want to brave the local cuisine, but definitely don't swim in the sea, as it's polluted. And maybe avoid the ear-cleaning "doctors" with their six-inch, pointy steel pins while you're at it. I don't even want to think about what the eye washers get up to.

The Chor Bazaar is where serious antique hunters head to find bargains on Victorian furniture, Ming vases, and Murano glass chandeliers. No one is certain how it got the name Thieves Market (a literal translation of *chor bazaar*), but one theory is that wealthy arrivals to Bombay would lose their valuables during the unloading of the ship, only to find them hanging in the bazaar's famous Mutton Street the following day. True or not, Chor Bazaar is most certainly a place where stolen goods have been bought and sold over the decades, and for that reason it's best that the buyer beware when it comes to purchasing "authentic" pieces.

It'd be hypocritical to criticize Mumbai's lack of public toilets, since my hometown of Manhattan has even fewer public toilets than this city. There's a reason that women live on average of five years longer than men, which is to make up for the time we spent waiting to use a restroom. So the rules remain the same as for visiting Times Square on a Saturday night: always go before you depart the hotel or restaurant, because the lav you know is better than the one you don't; always carry a pack of wipes; and don't overhydrate while out and about.

For those who are mad about Buddhist history, archaeology, or spelunking, you don't want to miss the Ellora and Ajanta Caves, which are an overnight trip from Mumbai. Literary buffs will be interested to know that the imaginary Marabar Caves in E. M. Forster's *A Passage to India* were based on the author's visit to the Ellora Cave temples and also those in the Barābar hills. In the novel, this is the location of the famous (real or imagined) rape scene, and if searching for symbolism, one can easily connect the caves to the female form and their intricate decoration to the inscrutability of India.

If you're lukewarm about spending several days prowling caves, then you can get the CliffsNotes version in just a few hours by taking the ferry from South Mumbai to Elephanta Island to see one spectacular cave that is representative of the lot and a World Heritage Site to boot. Carved out of solid rock, the Elephanta Caves date back to 600 CE and were intended as a collection of shrines, courtyards, grand halls, and inner sanctums featuring sculpted Hindu gods and goddesses. The island also serves as a free-range petting zoo, with roaming dogs and their adorable puppies, cows, goats, chickens, stunning bird life, and monkeys. All seem to live in harmony to the point where one could start singing "The Bare Necessities" from *The Jungle Book* movie, but the monkeys are actually bandits who lie in wait to perform smash-and-grab robberies on tourists. Much like at other attractions, young men offer themselves as guides, but in this instance, part of their service is to protect you from the monkeys. It's an offer that should not be disregarded lightly. I'm not saying that tangling with a robber baron primate is actually dangerous, so much as being mugged by monkeys is one of those things that is so much funnier when it's happening to a friend while you capture the scene on video and upload it to YouTube.

Another tactic is to buy off the monkeys by giving them a banana or just about anything edible, since they're not that picky when it comes to plunder. I tossed them several small packs of Fig Newtons. The terrific thing about monkeys is that opposable thumb, and they're happy to do the unwrapping, which also buys you the necessary time to escape. The alternative is to make friends with one of the friendly island dogs, and the monkeys will steer clear of you, because dogs came out slightly above them in the food chain. However, you'll need to feed the dog something in order to establish this relationship. But these homeless dogs are awfully particular, and anything without meat content is deemed unacceptable.

Mumbai may be home to the stock exchange, but the lunch exchange is far more interesting. The Dabbawala system enables around two hundred thousand lunch boxes to be picked up by carriers each day from restaurants and homes and taken on heads, by bicycle, handcart, and train to a central sorting station, where a sophisticated scheme of numbers and colors (since most carriers are illiterate), routes them to their destination. The system has an error rate of about one in 16 million, which is far better than that of our stock exchange, speaking from my own clerical experience. However, the white-capped Dabbawala is slowly being put out of business by the easy availability of fast food, along with an increase in the number of working wives, mothers, and daughters.

All of India is suffering from the environmental challenges that face a populous and growing country, but the one facing the monotheistic Zoroastrian religion is rather unique. For centuries, the Zoroastrians have wrapped their dead in white muslin and left the bodies at the raised circular Tower of Silence on Mumbai's Malabar Hill to be devoured by vultures. According to the tenets of Zoroastrianism, this is the only way their souls can be freed, since they worship fire and therefore view cremation a mortal sin, and burial is considered a contamination of the sacred earth. However, the vultures are no longer showing up and doing their part. Millions of South Asian vultures have died over the past two decades from feasting on cattle carcasses tainted by a painkiller given to sick cows. Conservationists estimate that more than 90 percent of India's vultures have disappeared, creating something of a work stoppage with regard to the funeral rites of the Parsis (members of the Zoroastrian community). Three to four bodies arrive every day, and they're coated with lime in an effort to hasten decomposition, but this is a process that, sans vultures, can take several months, even longer during the rainy season. Let's just say that people are getting upset, especially since Malabar Hill has become one of Mumbai's toniest neighborhoods, and for some reason, residents don't care to have piles of rotting corpses in their backyard.

Another famous feature of Indian life may also be disappearing. One of the most pleasing sights is the millions of sari-clad women darting about who resemble brightly plumed birds. Saris are intended to be vibrant. Swirling yellow, green, and red are considered to be festive and good luck, and also helpful with regard to fertility. Red is used as a bridal color in many parts of the country. White is only for widows, since life without a husband is thought to be a life without color. Black is considered bad luck on its own and must be mixed with other colors, while blue suggests the life-giving force of the monsoon and the beautiful boy-god Krishna. Saris are often stitched together with metallic-colored threads and festooned with shiny rhinestones, trim, and appliqué. Add to that several pounds of chandelier earrings, jeweled necklaces, cocktail rings, bangle bracelets, gold anklets with brass bells, and coiled silver toe rings, and it's safe to say that bling-bling is right at home here. A girl fight would be very ugly indeed, and a female game of crack the whip could be downright deadly.

While traversing the streets of Indian cities, I saw a large number of young women dressed in Western-style clothes and said to my Mumbai guide that I thought perhaps the silk sari was going the way of the Full Cleveland, a plaid leisure suit with a wide white belt and white dress shoes that came in lime green, Ramada orange, and neon plum. He became indignant and insisted that the sari would always be worn by the women of India. I asked him about his mother, and he replied that she wore a sari all the time. His wife sometimes wore a sari, his teenage daughters not at all. "They wear jeans and T-shirts like you have on." As if to highlight the transition, I saw two trailblazing gals sporting saris underneath Hard Rock Cafe and Hello Kitty hoodies. The sari will survive the same way native dress has in Africa: for weddings, ceremonies, celebrations, special events, and, of course, putting on shows for tourists. However, modern saris feature an embroidered phone pocket just below the waist on the left.

Can you don a sari and go native, as the Brits liked to say? Absolutely. In fact, it's encouraged, and any number of shops will whip up a custom sari for you within a day. But trust me, you will feel silly. Wrapped like a burrito in green and gold silk, I looked as if I'd just returned from a spoon-bending party.

All Aboard!

If you guessed that Walmart, with its 1.8 million workers, is the largest employer in the world, you'd be correct, as far as private companies go. But Indian Railways is the second largest state employer, with more than 1.5 million workers. (The Chinese army is number one in manpower, with 2.3 million.) The British are credited with organizing this extensive rail system throughout India, which was considerate, but one can't overlook the fact that it's impossible to have a productive colony without a way to move your raw materials across wide expanses of desert, mountains, and jungle.

When one thinks of the railroad in India, what probably comes immediately to mind are Internet photos of overcrowded trains with people piled atop the cars, spilling out doorways, plastered against the locomotive, hanging off the sides, and clinging to window frames, which is jokingly referred to as "ninth class" and gives a whole new meaning to the words *mass transit*. Unfortunately, those pictures were not photoshopped but taken of actual Mumbai commuter trains that transport 7 million workers per day (imagine the entire population of London hopping on trains) back and forth from residential northern suburbs to jobs in the city. Rush hour congestion aboard these death traps, where dozens of riders are killed or maimed every month, should soon be eased as a result of the metro system and monorail that are currently under construction.

However, traveling by long-distance express train in an air-conditioned chair car or sleeper, where seats and berths are reserved, is a safe, convenient, inexpensive, and comfortable way to see India, if you have the time. There are also several luxury trains, such as the Maharajas' Express, the Deccan Odyssey, Golden Chariot, Palace on Wheels, and Splendor of the South, that do specialty tours.

Trains get booked up far in advance, so it's a necessity to make reservations via computer or travel agent several weeks beforehand, especially during the high season (October to May). However, a tourist quota exists, and therefore it is possible to check for train availability a day or two before your trip. Buying tickets at the train station involves a maddening maze of long lines rife with operators who want bribes, try to scalp real and imagined tickets, and specialize in misdirection for profit, so check with your hotel or a travel office. Or locate the tourist office in the train station, which the locals don't usually know about and the scam artists don't want you to know about.

I reserved a berth on the Mandovi Express, which meanders down the West Coast from Mumbai to Goa and is supposed to take fourteen hours. However, don't be fooled by the word *express*—although the train doesn't stop at every village along the way, the switching system in India hasn't been updated so that two trains can pass each other in many places, and therefore you stop and wait in various locations. If you're twentysomething and backpacking, by all means go native and experience the world by purchasing a ticket in second or third class. For everyone else, here's the breakdown: an American had best book first class, since this is equivalent to what we'd think of as third class, while Indian second class is the equivalent of our camping, and their third class is on par with our correctional facilities in the 1940s.

The first question I was asked when booking a train ticket was my age. Odd. In middle middle age, I'm clearly not a child and not yet a senior citizen. Do the very young or the old and infirm have a lesser chance of completing the fourteen-hour journey? When I climbed aboard, was a conductor going to study my face and declare whether or not I looked good for my years?

Half the fun of rail travel is experiencing the train station. Much like Indian roads, things have not been separated in Indian train stations the way they are in the United States, with specific areas for passengers, cargo, animals, and vagrancy. People and stray dogs lie fast asleep among burlap sacks of grain, fifty-kilo bags of rice, coils of rope, rows of fresh lumber, rolled-up carpets secured with coconut-fiber twine, and wooden crates full of live chickens. Shoeshine boys ply their trade between forklifts piled with boxes of watermelon and idle scooters. It's the endless mishmash of an enormous flea market, except in the case of the ladies waiting room, which, while neither tidier than the rest of the station nor offering any particular amenities, provides a safe place where women and girls can eat, relax, and sleep with their modesty intact.

Mumbai's Chhatrapati Shivaji Terminus railway station, which is still known by its former official name, Victoria Terminus (or VT for short), is a vast, Gothic cathedral-like complex with stained-glass windows, flying buttresses, pointy turrets, soot-covered friezes, and vigilant gargoyles, overflowing with humanity, from commuters racing the clock to those in a deep slumber. Much like at midtown Manhattan's Penn Station, it can be hard to tell who is merely awaiting the arrival of a train and who receives mail there. Nonetheless, there was no begging, hawking, loud noise, molestation, or unpleasantness of any kind. Amazingly, the thousands of people walking, waiting, or just being in the enormous hall were all courteous, quiet, and respectful. Best of all, there's no need to set an alarm if you have to be at work or catch an early train, since the crowing roosters will do the job.

If anything, waiting in the Mumbai train station was akin to sitting in a large, unisex gym locker room. The main business of this transportation hub appears to be attention to personal hygiene. Hundreds of men and a few women were busy changing clothes, some going into the lavatory to do so and others not. It's like watching a pantomime, since the entire process is accomplished quietly, although not unobtrusively. Almost everyone carried a towel, bar of soap, and, in some cases, a deodorant stick. Dozens of men even strolled to and from the lav with towels wrapped around their waists. Women came out with fresh faces, combing just-washed hair. There was a certain amount of ceremony to the proceedings, as clothes and towels were carefully folded and then neatly tucked away.

The lavs were actually not that bad, and certainly no haven for any sort of inappropriate behavior. A sari-clad female attendant swabbing the floor with a mop had bare feet, as if daring you to question the cleanliness of her domain. Honestly, I've seen worse public facilities at major tourist attractions in Italy, New York's Port Authority, Union Station in Washington, DC, most Greyhound bus stations, and Girl Scout camp circa 1976.

Once you've found your place on the train, don't bother searching for the buffet, dining, or bar car, since there isn't one. If you're traveling first class, food is included in your fare, and the attendant will come to take your order. Whether you want to eat what's on offer is another matter. Many people bring their own food, which is probably a safe bet. Whereas the largest gamble in Las Vegas is said to be the ninety-nine-cent shrimp cocktail, the word on the tracks is to steer clear of the coconut chutney. This is often diluted with water to make it go further, the way that large families in my neighborhood added Quaker Oats to stretch the meatloaf, only this filler wasn't harmful to your health.

You'll soon hear the chai wallah's hypnotic shout of "*Chai, chai, garam chai*," breaking the word *chai* into separate syllables, "chai-eeee," as he makes his way through the cars offering milky sweet tea. *Chai* is actually the Hindi word for "tea." And a wallah is a person who performs a certain task, thus you have chai wallahs selling tea, rickshaw wallahs driving rickshaws, bidi wallahs hawking cigarettes, the cable wallah, the coal wallah, and nowadays the all-important wedding video wallah. The Chinese wallah, as it happens, is not Chinese, nor does he sell Chinese, but is in fact an Indian vendor of Chinese food.

Tea is the number one beverage in India and keeps the populace going the way Red Bull does college students in the United States. India is the world's largest consumer, second-largest producer, and fourth-largest exporter of tea. Chai wallahs are on every corner and encourage customer loyalty by using specialty ingredients, such as a pinch of crushed ginger, a dollop of cardamom, or a strand of saffron. Or by creating a bit of performance art by swirling the pot until it almost boils over, sweeping it back and forth between two pots several feet apart, and then sending a thin stream of chai into a brown clay cup held as far away as possible. In the movie *Slumdog Millionaire,* the game show contestant is referred to as a chai wallah, and the character who stars in *Salaam Bombay* also works as a chai wallah.

As you pull into most railway stations, the train is greeted by newspaper wallahs, fruit peddlers, and numerous vendors pushing their wares, including toiletries, eggs, vinyl belts, bottled water, tobacco, and toys for children. In the evening, you'll be supplied with clean sheets to cover your bunk, along with a blanket and pillow. Most first-class compartments have four sleeping berths. Is it possible to end up stretched out above or across from a man you've never seen before who reeks of chickpea curry and wants to talk all night long? Yes, indeed. Is it a little weird? Absolutely.

Still, on a train trip you quickly come to see how social, polite, and hospitable Indians are, as it feels like one big group hug. People are so amiable that it's difficult to tell in the midst of so much happy haphazardness which clusters are friends or families traveling together and who just met on board. It's not treated as a federal offense to use someone else's bag as a headrest or for a child's arm to flop across a stranger's lap.

Passengers don't scowl or grumble as you climb over them and push past to find the lav.

Whereas we have *good morning, good afternoon, good evening,* and *good night,* Indians use *namaste* for all that and more, much the way Hawaiians put *aloha* to work as a utility player. The word *namaste* derives from Sanskrit and roughly translated means, "I bow to the divinity that is inherent within you." The Hindi word *kal* means "yesterday" and also "tomorrow." Sorting out these last two can solve a lot of transportation problems before they happen.

Indians smile almost continuously while talking and ask lots of questions about you and your travels and what kind of family you have and about the country you're from. It's rather the opposite of France, where it's considered rude to ask personal questions of people who are merely acquaintances or that you meet in passing. Or Cuba, where locals strike up conversations with the aim of getting married that evening and moving back to the United States with you. Not surprisingly, just as we have preconceived notions of India, so do Indians of the States, mostly from shows like *Desperate Housewives* and *Baywatch* (perpetually in rerun), where we're not shown in our most intellectual light. Also, Indian men who look at porn see a great deal of American content, and this leads them to believe that at least half of the young American women they meet work in adult entertainment and will welcome their flirtations.

When discussing America, I always tried to give a balanced view, that there's plenty of opportunity—look how Barack Obama's mother was collecting welfare at one point and now he's president—but we also have problems with drugs and violence and a high rate of teen pregnancy. After that, all anyone ever wanted to talk about was teen pregnancy. It would seem that abstinence hasn't exactly worked in India either, based on the fact that the country's population has skyrocketed from 435 million in 1960 to 1.2 billion today. In other words, flash mobs are redundant.

Down South

India has forty-seven hundred miles of coastline and the South is the place to enjoy lolling on white sand beaches and canoeing through tropical rainforests that haven't changed in more than a thousand years. As a matter of fact, some tribal people live in the forest much as they did a century ago, and when the modern-age Department of Forestry encroaches on their resources and lifestyle, they'll take thirty or forty of them hostage to protest. I was reminded of the toxic chemicals seeping to the surface in Western New York's Love Canal neighborhood in the seventies and how frustrated locals took a few EPA workers captive. Soon afterward, Love Canal became the first Superfund cleanup site in the nation.

Goa is India's smallest state and is most famous for being the laid-back hippie hacienda of the sixties. During the Earth Shoe era, every free-thinking, dope-smoking, magic-bus-riding, tie-dyed- and denim-clad hippie in the world seemed to wash up on Goa's mystical shores for full-moon parties fueled by psychedelic drugs and exceedingly casual sex, much to the horror of its residents. Many died of overdoses or went home when their trusts funds ran out. Some stayed. But now you're more likely to find HUGs—hippies until college graduation—who will soon shed their L.L.Bean backpacks and become professionals, though possibly with a yen for hashish brownies. The occasional flash of a rusting orange-and-white Volkswagen van abandoned in the jungle still catches the eye, while the Anjuna market, better known as the hippie flea market, keeps the smell of sandalwood incense alive for newcomers.

Goa is the perfect place to get outfitted in colorful loose-fitting clothes and groovy jewelry, acquire some body piercings, visit the dreadlock creator, and tie on some smoky quartz crystals so you're ready for the techno music trance parties that begin around midnight and rave until dawn. Nearby boutiques and workshops sell wonderful handcrafted cane furniture and hand-painted ceramic tiles. Goa remains a heavily marketed tourist destination around the world, with clever taglines such as "Have fun in Goa" and "Give it a Goa."

The Portuguese landed in Goa in the early 1500s to seek Christian converts and ply the spice trade (not necessarily in that order), and the area remained a colony until 1961, when Indian troops seized the territory. Goa features European-style buildings with red tile roofs and art nouveau balconies in various states of dilapidation. Among the baroque church courtyards and graceful public squares, which are distinctly lacking in human density for India, old folks still gossip in Portuguese before purchasing the codfish and garlic cloves needed to whip up a batch of *bacalhau*.

For me, arriving in Goa was like being transported back to the heavily Catholic Buffalo, New York, of the sixties, where a crucifix could be spotted around every corner and throngs of parochial school children wearing uniforms dotted every street corner. Instead of packing everyone in wood-paneled station wagons as we used to do, entire Indian families pile atop motorbikes with book bags flying in the breeze. Otherwise, taxis double as churches, with interiors covered in Holy Family holograms, a dashboard statue of Jesus dying on the cross, and Mother Mary peering from behind the rearview mirror. The Mary statues looked so woebegone that I couldn't help but wonder if she'd been hoping for a girl instead. All that was needed to be a kitchen in my old neighborhood was an apostles spoon collection, Ten Commandments place mats (Sunday school project), and a stained-glass Lord's Prayer hanging in the window. After two weeks in mostly Hindu India, this was indeed culture shock.

Goa is unique in that the area features bullfights as a result of its deep Iberian roots. However, these aren't the kind Ernest Hemingway wrote about, where the matador flashes a red cape at the bull (who arrives already pissed off because his testicles are tied) and taunts it until somebody gets gored or killed. These spectacles are more like raves in that word spreads underground and a group of people gather in a field around two bulls that are encouraged to fight each other, and the winner is declared when one runs away. Such fights are illegal because there's a tremendous amount of gambling involved, and they're also dangerous—if you took careful note of the logistics here, the people are in a *circle* around two bulls, and one *runs away*. Spectators are expected to quickly part for the bull, and so obviously these events are somewhat participatory and not for the fearful or infirm. Still, they're a regular attraction since the police are paid to look the other way, ideally not in the direction in which the bull is running.

There are museums and churches galore to explore around here, and you can't toss a coconut without hitting one. The Basilica de Bom Jesus houses the mummified remains of Goa's great saint, sixteenth-century missionary Francis Xavier, who is said to have had miraculous powers of healing. Actually, the church is more like the home to the remains of his remains, since his body made a few stops before finally landing in Goa. A Portuguese woman, overwhelmed by her encounter with the saint's corpse, bit off the little toe of his left foot and attempted to sneak it out of the church in her mouth back in 1554. This brings us to the right forearm, the one Xavier used to bless his converts, which was detached and dispatched to Rome around 1614. Another part of his arm bone went to Macau and has been making the rounds over there ever since. And seemingly just for the heck of it, a holy fingernail lies twelve miles to the east in the village of Chandor. Outside of Bom Jesus, it's possible to shop for healing aids such as prayer cards, candles, statuettes, religious medals, vials of holy water, and, if that's not enough, wax body parts. Cue the "Hallelujah" chorus.

Most of all, Goa is a great place to chill out and enjoy some warm sand after the endless bustle of city life. However, the tides can be dangerous, so it's best to swim in view of a lifeguard. Dogs will stop by and inquire if you have a sandwich that you're not going to eat or a Coke can that needs peeing on. I saw hundreds of free-roaming dogs in half a dozen different cities across India, and oddly enough they appeared to be from the same litter, all with long noses, short hair, upturned ears, and weighing about forty-five pounds. In short, they all looked like dingoes. I don't call them wild dogs since they're friendly and outgoing and appear to have made a pact with the general populace with regard to mooching food and being permitted to laze around in exchange for remaining on good behavior, so perhaps *liberated* is a better term.

I was also in the country long enough to observe that public places such as airports, malls, and hotel lobbies seem to favor instrumental versions of 1970s American movie soundtracks over traditional Indian music. In particular, the melodic strains of Marvin Hamlisch's theme song "The Last Time I Felt Like This" from the American film *Same Time, Next Year* appear to be all the rage, whether you're ordering Goan egg curry or having henna applied. I'm guessing the DJ in charge doesn't know that the movie is about adultery.

On the beaches in the South, you'll be approached by women wearing exquisite silk saris who are peddling scarves, shawls, and jewelry. However, it's a soft sell, and although most never went very far in school, if they attended at all, the English they've learned solely from conversing with tourists is impressive, along with their Italian, French, Spanish, Russian, and smattering of Japanese. In fact, their language capabilities and interpersonal skills greatly exceeded those of the men working in most of the good hotels, yet they were earning 1/100th of the pay. If it's a slow day, the women will happily chat and ask you about your family, and if you're interested in their lives, they'll tell you everything you'd like to know.

Although the cows in Goa appear to be independent operators, in reality they're ladies who lunch. The gals leave home in the morning to visit friends, graze, apply a mud mask, and sunbathe by the roadside while catching up on all the gossip, and then return to their abodes in the evening.

Tourists usually head to the North of India and travel no further south than Jaipur, but the South is now a real contender. The success of information, biotechnology, and pharmaceutical companies in Bangalore, Hyderabad, Pune, and Chennai (formerly Madras) have brought economic success, while social progress resulting from a meritocracy based on education (as opposed to nepotism and the caste system) have made it a wonderful place for travelers to enjoy. Hyderabad is in fact nicknamed Cyberabad because of the new infrastructure, five-star hotels, fashionable restaurants, and global companies that have been building state-of-the-art glass-walled campuses and skyscrapers throughout the city. Business people are in such a hurry to get there that flights leave from Mumbai starting at three in the morning.

Located to the south of Goa is the historic seaport city of Kochi (formerly Cochin) in the state of Kerala, which is known as the Venice of the East. This group of islands shares a mixed heritage, as evidenced by the enormous Chinese fishing nets on display at the tip of Fort Cochin (which contains just about every type of monument except a proper fort) that were introduced by traders from the court of Kublai Khan around 1400 CE, Saint Francis Church, constructed in 1503, Portuguese Mattancherry Palace, built in 1555, and the (Protestant) Dutch Cemetery, which was consecrated in 1724. As if that's not cultural crossroads enough,

Mattancherry Palace shares a wall with the Paradesi Synagogue. Built in 1568, this is India's oldest synagogue and is located in an area with the bouncy name of Jew Town. The first wave of Jews arrived in India following the capture of Jerusalem in 587 BCE and settled in Cochin. Paradesi Synagogue contains a number of antiquities worth visiting, including a floor composed of hundreds of eighteenth-century hand-painted porcelain tiles (which, according to the caretaker, Queen Elizabeth II claimed to adore on her 1997 visit and kvetched about how they're impossible to find nowadays), a number of stunning Belgian chandeliers, and an Oriental rug that was a gift from Ethiopian emperor Haile Selassie I. Despite being an Ethiopian Orthodox Christian, Selassie traced his roots back to Solomon, a King of Israel, according to the Hebrew Bible. Meantime, the Rastafarian movement in Jamaica was built upon the premise that Selassie was a messianic figure destined to lead the African people into a new era of peace, righteousness, and prosperity. Talk about being different things to different people.

A day trip from Kochi is the tranquil riverside village and popular picnic spot of Kodanad. This rural hamlet was once the largest capturing camp in South India for elephants that would be sold to circuses, zoos, and private game preserves, but hunting was made illegal in 1977, and so the camp has been converted into a rescue and care center. It's also a tourist destination, with river walks and the opportunity to ride elephants, visit the babies, and, if you're prepared for full-contact and complete submersion, a plunge into the river to give an elephant a bath using a coconut husk as a loofah.

Other popular attractions in the South include Mysore's Maharaja Palace; the temple ruins and giant boulders of Hampi; Ooty, so stunningly beautiful that the British named it Queen of the Hill Stations; and Puducherry (formerly Pondicherry), on the East Coast, which retains a delightful Gallic atmosphere, having been an on-again off-again colony of France until 1954.

Between Puducherry and Chennai is Mamallapuram (popularly known as Mahabalipuram), the ancient port city of the Pallava kings (rulers of the south from the fourth to ninth century CE) and a showcase of architectural wonders. Its rock-cut caves, friezes, temples, and bas-relief sculpted artwork, constructed mostly between the seventh and ninth centuries, are a sight to behold. The Shore Temple is dramatically floodlit at night and is probably the second most photographed monument in India after the Taj Mahal. Meantime, if you've been thinking about a four-armed Lord Shiva statue for the entranceway back home or an elephant-headed Ganesha to top off the garden, Mal (as it's called) is a great place to purchase a stone carving. Mal's fine local chiselers are regularly commissioned to create sculptures for new temples being built around the world. After haggling over the price, scratch your name on the bottom and request that it be shipped home. Mamallapuram is also a backpackers' paradise, so expect the requisite Internet cafés, coconut sellers, food stalls, love beads, marigold garlands, aphrodisiacs, Bob Marley T-shirts, and what must surely be faux iPhones, based on the price. If you're looking for a good place to have a midlife crisis, Mal could indeed be the ticket.

In the southeastern state of Tamil Nadu, there are bull-taming festivals between January and May as a part of Pongal, the harvest celebration. Rules differ from place to place, but the ritual, known as jallikattu, usually involves trying to hang onto the hump of a colorfully decorated, fast-running bull for a predetermined amount of time. In another version, unarmed villagers attempt to gain possession of a bundle of cash that's been tied to the bulls' sharpened horns. The animals are not killed, like in Spanish bullfighting, but more than two hundred participants have died over the past twenty years, and thousands have sustained injuries. Opponents of the sport, which they call bull baiting, object to the fact that the bulls have chili pepper rubbed in their eyes, are force-fed alcohol, and have their male parts pinched in order to rile them up sufficiently.

However, it seems the critics are outsiders, since locals all told me that the bull-taming sessions are an important part of their culture and history. Apparently, a wealthy prince could easily and efficiently sort through competing potential sons-in-law by putting them to the test. And so residents are put out by interlopers wanting to interfere, the way Buffalonians don't like Floridians making fun of their blizzards, and people actually from Detroit are the only ones allowed to brag that they make the best car thieves.

In the end, it might be good old-fashioned Western-style ambulance chasing that redefines this increasingly controversial tradition. Villages wanting to hold bull-taming festivals are now required to put down large deposits since victims and their families are starting to demand compensation for accidents and injuries.

I'd be able to tell you more about all of that, but several days of monsoon rains (heavy to very heavy rains, according to the local newscaster) ripped through the South and slightly altered my plans. Much the way Western New York has two seasons, allergy and flu, India has tourist and monsoon. So I'll leave off with some fluid dynamics factoids: Whereas buses and taxis tend to sink in large quantities of water, wooden rickshaws do not.

Q: Do cows float?
A: Yes.
Q: Do pregnant cows float?
A: Especially so.

So Many Gods,
So Little Time

India is a predominantly Hindu country (83 percent of the population), but out of 1.2 billion people, that still leaves several hundred thousand, and therefore one can also find a good many Muslims (11 percent), Christians (2.5 percent), Sikhs (2 percent), Buddhists (about 1 percent), and Jains (less than 1 percent), along with a smattering of Parsis, Baha'is, and Jews. With about 177 million Muslims in total, India has the third-largest Muslim population after Indonesia (204 million) and Pakistan (178 million). Aside from occasional outbreaks of violence, India's Muslim communities are not associated with terrorist activities. In fact, the country's wealthiest man is a Muslim, as are many highly placed government officials and popular film stars. Muslim men and women are allowed by law to fully function within this democracy, and all have a vote. Membership in a minority religion does not impede advancement in business, politics, or the professions. At least three Indian presidents and three chief justices have been Muslim. Many prominent lawyers and doctors have been Muslim, Christian, and Parsi. In fact, not long ago, India had a Muslim president, a Sikh prime minister, and a Congress party leader who was Christian, all democratically elected in a country with a Hindu majority. Furthermore, no one has declared that there's a war on Christmas, Holi, Wesak, Ramadan, or Hanukkah. Now that's diversity.

Hinduism, which has more than 800 million followers, encompasses a wide range of beliefs and practices. A PBS program explaining Hinduism is going to run substantially longer than the Richard Gere–narrated two-hour PBS special on Buddhism. Hinduism has no single sacred text, dogma, founder, prophet, or worship schedule. What is clear to the outside observer is that Hindus don't eat beef, although chicken and fish are okay. Otherwise, the basic idea is that the human soul is considered to be everlasting and in a perpetual state of development, so reincarnation is an important element of the Hindu faith. After death, the soul is born again on earth in a new form, with the purpose of bettering itself until perfection is attained. Rebirth is governed by karma, which states that we regularly have a choice between good and evil, and each decision will impact our future experiences accordingly. There is also the idea that the sins of our past life will be visited upon us in our next life. It can hardly be a coincidence that both doctrines uphold my kindergarten teacher's second-favorite expression, "We reap what we sow," which came directly after "Just because you *can* say anything you want doesn't mean that you should."

Although we usually employ the word *karma* in a philosophical sense in the West—what comes around goes around, cast your bread upon the waters, and so forth—in India, the belief discourages people from attempting to cross caste lines for social relations and therefore isn't entirely in tune with modernity. Likewise, dharma, the obligation to accept one's condition and perform the duties appropriate to it, puts a burden on the poor or low caste and gives the rich and those of high caste a license to behave in a superior manner, ignore the plight of the downtrodden, and take privileges, such as cutting in line and taking the best seats.

Hinduism is about as far from monotheism as you can get, since instead of one god there are literally thousands of gods and goddesses, most with their own personal modes of conveyance, not unlike the modern-day Popemobile. One has to be born a Hindu, so don't worry about anyone pushing leaflets into your hand or ringing the doorbell and wanting to tell you what a friend he has in Vishnu. But this doesn't mean you can't dive headlong into Hinduism, since it has a considerable emphasis on personal religion. Most of the thousands of ashrams all across India, where holy men teach visitors in small groups, are Hindu affiliated. Yoga and meditation and sometimes a diet regimen can also be offered as elements of the spiritual journey. Yoga was originally developed by men and continues to be practiced by men in India, from regular working folk to weightlifters, so be prepared to see eighty-year-old guys knocking out handstands, backbends, the flying crow, and the one-legged king pigeon. In fact, former prime minister Jawaharlal Nehru regularly engaged in long conversations while standing on his head. Indian men are also known for being world-record holders in the category of longest fingernails and thus are way ahead of the United States when it comes to the whole metrosexual craze.

Interestingly, there's a group of Indian Americans who have recently mounted a Take Back Yoga campaign, as if the lotus position is under siege like Christmas decorations in public squares. Much like the Take Back America campaign it raises some obvious questions (from whom?). Take Back Yoga crusaders don't require practitioners to take up Hinduism or even study the religion but want devotees to recognize that the philosophy of yoga was first described in Hindu texts. (Although it would appear that yoga's roots can be traced back to before the start of Hinduism.) Still, it seems to me like trying to take back peppermint chewing gum, butter brickle ice cream, or plain old fire. The downward-facing dog genie is out of the bottle.

Yoga began as a sex cult, according to *The Science of Yoga*, a fascinating new book by American author William J. Broad, which gives an account of what yoga can and cannot do to heal the body and mind. Reports show that yoga may cause a surge of sex hormones that can improve the love lives of both men and women, writes Broad, while advanced yogis can close their eyes and light up their brains in states of ecstasy indistinguishable from sexual climaxes or (you knew it was coming) yogasms.

The red circle that a Hindu woman wears in the middle of her forehead is called a *bindi*, which is Sanskrit for "drop" or "dot." This effect used to be created through the application of a red powder, but nowadays disposable peel-and-stick bindis are available in a wide range of colors, including ones that sparkle like disco balls. The red-hued bindi originally symbolized marriage but has become mostly decorative, the equivalent of a butterfly tattoo above your butt or a handgun in America.

When India became an independent nation in 1947 and formed its own constitution, a certain amount of leeway had to be allowed for existing religious traditions with regard to birth, marriage, and death, and thus Muslims in India can practice polygamy. It's also practiced by a small percentage of Hindus, along with some Buddhists and Adivasi (also known as tribal or aboriginal groups). Among the

Hindu and Buddhist communities in northern India's Himalayan valley, which is notable for its harsh living conditions, you occasionally find polyandry, where a woman has several husbands. In such situations, one may wonder how it is known which children belong to which father. This is decided by the mother, and apparently whatever she says goes, and there's no such thing as paternity tests. However, polyandry is dying out as these communities become less isolated, more educated, and have increased access to earning opportunities. Interestingly, in plural-marriage societies, as a male gains wealth and stature, he wants more wives, whereas when a woman improves her lot, she apparently desires fewer husbands. Go figure.

Islam is a one-god shop, like Christianity and Judaism, and as with those religions, followers have divided into various degrees of devoutness, from Muslim-in-name-only to peace-loving practitioner and productive member of society, all the way to militant jihadist. A Muslim has five duties: believe in one God with Mohammad as his prophet, pray five times a day, fast from dawn until dusk during Ramadan, perform charitable acts, and make a pilgrimage to Mecca at least once. Islam can be a bit like the mail-order Columbia Record Club of the 1980s in that once you signed up it was difficult to unwind the relationship. To become a Muslim, one need only declare in front of an Islamic official, "There is no God but Allah, and

Mohammed is his prophet." However, to exit Islam is illegal and, among some sects, punishable by death.

Sharia (Islamic law) enforces differences between the roles of men and women with regard to marriage, divorce, legal status, dress code, and education that vary from place to place and family to family. Women have built careers and even achieved high political office in Muslim majority states, but many are prevented from realizing their academic and professional potential because of sharia, despite arguments that the Koran clearly states that men and women are equal.

Sikhism arose in the northern Punjab region during the fifteenth century and nowadays includes elements of both Islam and Hinduism. However, Sikhs aren't considered Hindus or Muslims, and their main goal is the union with (just one) god. Male Sikhs are easily identifiable by their turbans and heavy metal bracelets, and they're also required to carry a dagger, just FYI. If you enjoyed studying sets and subsets in seventh-grade math, here's one: Sikhs are all Singhs but not all Singhs are Sikhs. *Singh* means "lion," and all male Sikhs have this component in their name, while many Sikh women have *Kaur* in their name, which means "princess." At any given time, there are about forty Singhs in the Lok Sabha, the directly elected lower house of Parliament, which currently contains 545 members, including a speaker. Trying to find a specific Singh must be like trying to locate a particular

Vinny at the Feast of San Gennaro. On the plus side, it's easy to be polite, since any time a man with a turban helps you it's possible to say, "Thank you, Mr. Singh."

Sikhs have much in common with the Italians in Bensonhurst, Brooklyn, in that they pay a lot of attention to their hair, think yoga is for sissies, and have a reputation for being very tough, so don't mess with them. In American movies and sitcoms such as *Outsourced*, the Sikh typically ends up playing "the scary-looking guy." Sikhs are also like the Chinese in America in that you never see them begging on the streets, which leads one to assume that they take care of their own. In addition to being community minded, they're generous to outsiders, and therefore Sikh temples offer meals to thousands of people from all walks of life every day of the year. Sikhs aren't supposed to eat meat slaughtered in a cruel manner, drink alcohol, use tobacco, or commit adultery and are commonly mistaken for Muslims, especially by Westerners.

Sikhs deserve a big shout-out for incorporating into their religious bylaws that a Sikh woman is equal to a Sikh man and that the souls of women and men are the same, therefore women can participate equally in all religious, cultural, and social activities, including the leading of congregations. Does this mean that Sikhism provides women with an oasis of liberation? No. Local traditions and social mores remain strong, the way they do everywhere until enough people say enough is enough. I'm reminded of my Western New York public school, where we said a pledge every morning to a single god (no matter that students might be atheist or polytheist), fish was served every Friday for the benefit of the many Catholics, we sang mostly Christian music in chorus despite the presence of a dozen or so Jews, girls were issued "previously enjoyed" boys' soccer uniforms since our sporting endeavors apparently didn't merit splurging for something new with darts and other concessions to the female form, and we were bused to an elementary school gym for practice so as not to scuff the precious floor of the boys' gym.

The spiritual center and holiest shrine of Sikhism is the Golden Temple in Amritsar, not far from the border of Pakistan. This gleaming gold and polished marble complex is a popular destination for celebrities and politicians. Even Queen Elizabeth II and Prince Philip have padded around in their stockinged feet. However, President Obama, a Christian, was advised to skip this stop on his 2010 India trip because wrapping a cloth around his head would have fueled rumors that he's a Muslim. The act of tying has spiritual significance for the Sikhs, and thus a Chicago White Sox baseball cap was not an acceptable compromise.

Buddhism, like Hinduism, originated in India. It's the world's fourth-largest religion and is centered around the search for inner peace, which usually involves practicing hours of meditation on the road to enlightenment. Buddhism is, of course, the religion of the Dalai Lama, with whom most of us are familiar as a result of the political situation whereby Tibet, Buddhist HQ, is being claimed by the Chinese. Or because we watched *Caddyshack* several hundred times, where Carl the groundskeeper, played by Bill Murray, supposedly caddied for the Dalai Lama and in lieu of a cash tip received eternal consciousness on his deathbed, at which point he states, "So I figure I got that going for me."

Technically speaking, His Holiness retired on March 14, 2011, but his followers didn't take it very seriously. It was like my friend Mary's house, where there were nine kids and her mother used to throw her hands up and "quit" at least once a month, but all the kids showed up at the dinner table just the same. As a result, his formal title changed from Head of Nation to Protector and Symbol of Tibet and Tibetan People. More importantly, by installing an elected prime minister, the Dalai Lama is betting that democracy might prevent China from claiming Tibet after his death.

Meantime, the Chinese have decided on their own candidate to fill the Dalai Lama's saffron-and-maroon robes. However, he threw some ferocious logic at them: as Communist atheists, they can't possibly believe in reincarnation and therefore cannot identify the next Dalai Lama. I wouldn't want to play chess against that guy. And I'll bet he does crossword puzzles in ink.

Fun fact: The current Dalai Lama, who was born July 6, 1935, and took the throne at age five, has served his followers longer than such long-lasting rulers as Queen Elizabeth II , King Rama IX of Thailand, and Fidel Castro.

The Buddha, or "Enlightened One," was Siddhārtha Gautama, who lived in the sixth century BCE. Siddhārtha was the son of a Hindu ruler of a small kingdom in the Nepalese foothills and a member of the warrior caste. Raised in a sheltered atmosphere with plenty of servants, his life was one of luxury and comfort. However, a fortune-teller predicted that because of his concern for human suffering, Prince Siddhārtha would one day forsake the world, and so his father ordered that he be shielded from pain and unpleasantness. Nonetheless, Siddhārtha gradually became aware of the sorrow and affliction in people's lives and set out to fix things. At the age of twenty-nine, he renounced the palace lifestyle, his wife, and his young child. Siddhārtha dressed as a hermit, and since it was not yet possible to join the Peace Corps and build irrigation ditches, he set out on a journey to seek spiritual truth, timeless wisdom, and the secret of sorrow. But despite his asceticism and deprivations, Siddhārtha failed and sat meditating under the Bodhi tree at Bodh Gaya, near Benares (now Varanasi). After forty-nine days, enlightenment finally dawned, the meaning of sorrow became clear, and he preached his first sermon. The essential message was that sorrow is the cause of all the evil and suffering in the world. Because pain and bad behavior arise from unhealthy desires (basically, anything that doesn't involve yearning for enlightenment), each individual must start tearing up his wish list and learn selflessness. By not having any local priests, Buddhism provides a less hierarchical way of life for all of its practitioners, so you tend not to encounter leaders with television stations, theme parks, private jets, and monasteries full of designer clothing.

More importantly, why are there so many statues of a fat, bald, laughing Buddha for sale at every kiosk when Siddhārtha Gautama was supposedly tall, serene, and slender? Just as there's more than one guy in the American South named Bubba, there are a number of men called Buddha in the East. The jolly, heavyset "rub my belly for good luck" Buddha is most likely a depiction of an eccentric Chinese monk who lived during the Later Liang Dynasty. However, there are conflicting stories and it's possible that after Buddhism's Buddha achieved perfect enlightenment, he may have rewarded himself with too many slices of triple chocolate bliss cake.

Today, Buddhism has an appealing ambassador in the exiled Dalai Lama (a Mongolian name that means "Ocean of Wisdom") along with sensible, easy-to-understand tenets, such as: be cool, exercise moderation, do the right thing, no pain no gain, respect nature, try to leave the world better than you found it, and beware of the butterfly effect—that actions cause other actions. So think before you act, or as my friend likes to tell her four-year-old, "Make good decisions." Like most religions, Buddhism has parables. When a mother loses her only son and takes his body to the Buddha to restore the boy, he tells her to go from house to house and bring back a handful of mustard seed from a family that never lost a child, husband, parent, or friend. When the mother is unable to find such a house in her village, she realizes that death is common to all and she can't be selfish in her grief. In other words, it's not suffering, but our response to suffering, that defines who we are. Buddhism also serves up lots of proverbs, such as "When the student is ready, the teacher will appear," and "If we are facing the right direction, all we have to do is keep on walking."

Despite their regard for all sentient beings, Buddhists aren't required to be vegetarians. In fact, the omnivorous Dalai Lama enjoys bacon and eggs for breakfast, roast veal for lunch, and a good flank steak dinner. He also prefers to wear black leather Doc Martens instead of grass-rope sandals. In general, Buddhism is not a religion of rigidity, and therefore anyone is welcome to join at any time just by deciding that they like what they see. No trial by fire, immersion in water, financial contribution, or pledge of allegiance is required. Likewise, there's no punishment for deserters.

My only complaint about Buddhism is that the Dalai Lama has always been a man. You don't see the monks assigned to scour the countryside for the next incarnation of the Dalai Lama looking into the souls of any young girls, not even a tree-climbing tomboy. Thus there will be no Dalai Mama or Lama Mama, and this sends the wrong message to girls—that men are closer to god/truth than women, and for all its promise of hope and healing, this religion's top job can never be yours. Young women already have enough catching up to do, especially in that part of the world. From my lips to the leader's ears—the current but retired Dalai Lama has stated that the next Buddhist leader *could* be a girl. (Get the Pope on line one.) Otherwise, for better or worse, Buddhism does not appear to be a religion that inspires much musical theater along the lines of *Fiddler on the Roof*, *Nunsense*, or *The Book of Mormon*. Come to think of it, I haven't even heard a Buddhist joke since fifth grade, when this thigh-slapper was making the rounds: "What did Buddha say to the hot dog vendor?" Answer: "Make me one with everything."

One last thought regarding Buddhism: Can a religion be too passive? When traveling in Cambodia after their civil war, in the seventies, I stayed at a hotel with a swimming pool that had, up until several weeks earlier, been filled with dead bodies. A foreign correspondent from Dallas leaned over and said that the reason mass murder on such an enormous scale (2 million people) happened in the first place was because the Cambodians were too submissive as a result of their Buddhist beliefs. He insisted that none of this could have occurred in Texas, because the first person the Khmer Rouge approached would've taken a handgun from her purse or a shotgun from his roof rack, blown the guy's hat off, and carried on down the highway to the armadillo races, thereby nipping the whole genocide thing in the bud.

Interestingly, a lot of Hindus jump ship for Buddhism because Buddhism doesn't maintain or recognize the caste system, and therefore in one fell swoop a person can cast off generations of caste. Buddhism also seems to be the practice that appeals most to Westerners, in particular twentysomething New York Jews requiring a change of religious scenery before getting married and having children and rejoining the faith of their forefathers, or else heading over to the Society for Ethical Culture. It also appealed to German composer Richard Wagner, who incorporated Buddhist themes in his operas *Tristan und Isolde* and *Parsifal*. As for the general populace dashing off to the nearest monastery, no less than the retired Dalai Lama himself has concluded that it's easier to stay put. "Better not take someone else's religion—it is better to stick with the wisdom traditions of one's own land than to run from them, pursuing in exotica what was under your nose all the time."

Jainism is distinct for its self-discipline, its tradition of scholarship, and, most famously, its belief in nonviolence toward all living things. On top of being vegetarian, Jains don't eat root vegetables such as potatoes and onions, since the bulb is considered a living being, and they don't use honey since the collection process is considered to be violence against bees. They aren't supposed to smoke or use any addictive substances, including alcohol.

In addition to the hospital for birds in Delhi, the Jains operate shelters for cows and even a home for insects in the city of Ahmadabad. One faction of Jain monks cover their mouths to avoid swallowing bugs and sweep the paths in front of them so as to avoid stepping on any creepy crawlies. Oddly enough, for a religion that's so absorbed with preserving life, Jains have one of the highest gaps between giving birth to boys and girls, which means about 15 percent of the girls are victims of infanticide or gender determination followed by abortion. Oops.

Zoroastrianism is a religion and philosophy based on the teachings of Zoroaster, also known as Zarathustra. It entails the belief in one god, Ahura Mazda, along with a very *Star Wars*-like concept of light and dark where focusing on good thoughts and deeds is necessary to keep away chaos. Practitioners of the faith are also known as Parsis, since they originally came from Persia, now Iran, to escape persecution by

Muslims. The main thing to remember about Zoroastrianism is that Freddie Mercury, lead singer of the rock band Queen and composer of such hits as "Bohemian Rhapsody" and "We Are the Champions," was a Parsi originally named Farrokh Bulsara. Often referred to as Britain's first Asian rock star, Mercury was born in Zanzibar (Tanzania, Africa) and was raised there and in India before moving to England at the age of seventeen. India hasn't capitalized on Freddie Mercury tourism the way that Zanzibar has, where you can go on all-day pilgrimages with people wearing red leather pants, silver-studded belts, and aviator glasses while "Barcelona" blares through the minivan speakers. Tours conclude at the beachfront restaurant named Mercury's, which features memorabilia, music, cocktails, and a full menu, including Freddie's Fruit Salad. One theory on why a full day is necessary is because service at the restaurant is so slow.

When European priests arrived in southern India during the 1500s to introduce Christianity, they were surprised to find that someone had beaten them to the task. None other than Saint Thomas, one of the original apostles (a.k.a. Doubting Thomas), had supposedly converted the first Indians after arriving aboard a Roman trading ship in 52 CE and was buried in Madras (now Chennai) after possibly being crucified. Ancient scrolls have Jesus living in India not once but twice, the first time between the ages of twelve and thirty, and again after the Resurrection, teaching the gospel in Kashmir. There aren't any reliable accounts to confirm such early history, but academics and theologians agree that Christianity has been in India almost as long as the religion has existed, and that the subcontinent is home to one of the oldest Christian communities in the world. Approximately 25 million Christians live in India, making it the country's third-largest religion.

I hope you're sitting down. Because there are actually several dozen congregations of Unitarian Universalists practicing in Mother India, which just goes to show that the country really can produce a few of absolutely everything. (Although being one of nine thousand congregants in a country of 1.2 billion makes being a UU in India rather akin to being a Sufi in the United States.) In India, the UUs tend to do more with a tribal god and all-day worship services, while American UUs are more concerned with getting out the vote and making it to brunch at a reasonable time, where an everything bagel easily passes for Holy Communion. Likewise, congregation names in America tend to be longer than those of Spanish kings and sound reminiscent of a 1970s band featuring the African thumb piano, such as The Congregation of Earth, Wind, and Harmony—an All-Inclusive Fragrance-Free Community Embracing the Dignity of Difference. However, the Unitarian minister Ralph Waldo Emerson was influenced by both Hindu and

Buddhist scriptures while tweaking his beloved transcendentalism, a philosophy so difficult to explain and understand that hardly anyone remains interested in it for very long or can even remember what the heck it is. Matters weren't helped by the fact that notable nineteenth-century transcendentalists couldn't agree on exactly what it was, and in his 1842 lecture "The Transcendentalist," Emerson suggested that it was actually impossible to attain in practice. That said, when I was growing up there wasn't a UU terrarium-building party that didn't feature Indian musician and composer Ravi Shankar playing his sitar, especially "Song from the Hills" and "Twilight Mood," which, by the way, are now available as cell phone ringtones.

Fun fact: Ravi Shankar is the father of the lovely and talented singer-songwriter Geethali Norah Jones Shankar, who officially changed her name to Norah Jones right before becoming a best-selling recording artist and multiple Grammy award winner. However, Ms. Jones doesn't like to talk about her father, because her folks split when she was young and she was raised by her mother in Fort Worth, Texas.

Let there be no misunderstanding, a political party of activists wants to make India a Hindu country the same way special interest groups want to make the United States a Christian nation. Meantime, bordering nations Pakistan and Bangladesh don't have much tolerance for those who aren't Muslim, and forget about Jews. I recently read that there are fewer than one hundred Jews in both Iraq and Egypt, and only one Jew left in Afghanistan. One Jew! You can't even create a sitcom with only one Jew, and forget about a stand-up comedy club. However, India has a thriving community of approximately fifteen thousand Jews, one quarter of whom live in Mumbai. And at the city's popular Indigo delicatessen, you can order bagels and lox with a shmear of cream cheese, onions, and capers on a toasted poppy-seed bagel (spelled *bahgel*) or a Reuben sandwich—cured pastrami, sauerkraut, and Swiss cheese on rye bread with Thousand Island dressing and gherkins. All that's missing are specialty dishes named after famous comedians or Broadway shows and waitstaff with an attitude. Although you do have to bring your own pickled tongue.

Otherwise, I didn't meet anyone who'd admit to being an atheist in India, though they are rumored to be out there, including some Communist Party members in the South. However, this is the kind of thing you'd want to keep under your hat, as you'd miss out on time off for dozens of holidays.

In addition to religion, astrology plays a powerful role in daily life. As a matter of fact, astrology carries such weight that Independence had to be brought forward a day, and hence you have *Midnight's Children* rather than *Twelve Noon's Kids*. Even today, many newspaper ads for brides and grooms request individual astrological charts, and people consult astrologers to find good travel times and especially auspicious days for weddings. This is a job for highly trained professionals, since the practice is filled with nuances and subtleties. For instance, a chirping cricket can be considered an omen of good luck or bad luck depending on the day. Astrology is also used in weather prediction, which could be why you often see television footage of people evacuating two days after the flooding. Along similar lines, before earthquakes and tsunamis, UFO sightings are reported to rise, and it's been suggested that the UFOs are trying to warn us about planetary positioning effects on the earth's tectonic plates and crust, or else may actually be causing the disasters. Wait while I go find my mood ring.

Superstition also runs rampant in India. It is believed that if any members of the Boya tribe remain overnight in the village of Pyalakurthy they won't wake up in the morning—the result of an ancient curse placed following a supposed killing spree. As a result, Boyas come to visit, do business, or work in the fields during the day, but make sure to bed down in a neighboring village. Meantime, in the sleepy hamlet of Aalavizhaampatti, it is widely believed that great misfortune will fall upon anyone who drinks liquor; the result of a long-ago promise made to some traveling gods. And it's a safe bet that if outsiders drink too much they won't be able to say the name of this village.

Furthermore, many Indians worry that someone might cast an evil eye or *nazar* upon them and take precautions against such an unwelcome occurrence. For instance, construction sites often display a demonic figure to ward off evil spirits. People also employ rings, bracelets, charms, necklaces, and body markings to cancel its effects. Women might wear a particular gemstone or an amulet shaped like a fish, an eye, or the infinity symbol. Good luck charms can often be found under the front fender or below the rearview mirror of even the most expensive automobiles. A pandit (Hindu priest) is often consulted to select favorable letters for parents to use to start a baby's name. Meantime, said baby often has black dots placed behind each ear, in the middle of the forehead, on the temples, and on the soles of his feet so that people won't notice the beauty of the child, which is considered to be bad luck. These markings are often maintained for a year. So don't worry that any black-polka-dotted babies you might see are carrying some sort of plague. It's more like a nationwide game of pin the dot on the baby.

Caste Away System

The Hindu caste system affects all aspects of Indian society, from the social to the political. Even though discrimination based on caste is now illegal, in many cases it's still used to determine who gets what job and who can associate with whom. There are all kinds of medieval tenets, such as that a high-caste person must be on a platform to address a low-caste person. When two young lovers of different castes elope and get caught, they're often murdered by the men in their families, sometimes set on fire, or cut up with knives. (Where is Mom? one has to ask.)

The caste system arrived with the invasion by Indo-Europeans (usually called Aryans) from the Caucuses (the border of Europe and Asia) in 1500 BCE. It's said that the four castes—Brahman, Kshatryias, Vaishyas, Sudras—were produced from the body of the god Brahma and later branched out into hundreds of subcastes that vary from region to region and were based on what type of work was done. The underlying idea here seems to be that it's easier to accept your lot in life if there's an explanation, particularly one so absolute as the will of the gods. My favorite caste nomenclature created by the central government is Other Backward Classes, to distinguish lower castes from the higher Forward Castes. Lower castes are broken down into backward, somewhat backward, and very backward, as opposed to the more *Sesame Street*-friendly low, lower, and lowest. The untouchables (also known as Dalits, meaning "the oppressed") are called Scheduled Caste instead of Outcaste, which is how they were historically viewed and treated. As a result of some bad karma in previous incarnations, untouchables were condemned to spend their lives emptying chamber pots, cleaning latrines, picking up trash, and dealing with corpses.

Mahatma Gandhi gave the untouchables the name Harijan, which means "God's people," as he was not a proponent of caste discrimination. Harijans shouldn't be confused with hijras, a nonhereditary grouping, or what we might call an alternative lifestyle, that includes transsexuals, transvestites, eunuchs, and intersexuals from every caste and religion. And this brings us to the conduct and treatment of another marginalized group.

The hijra have a social network second only to Facebook to find out the time and dates of weddings and childbirth celebrations (mostly for boys because a girl is considered to be a large financial liability and usually no cause for merriment) through a series of informants comprising sweepers, midwives, and *dho-bis* (laundrymen). Hijras put on makeup, dress up in saris, and arrive uninvited at parties to dance and bless. What amazes people is that no two groups show up at the same function, since various clusters of hijras have managed to divide up the whole of India like competing Mafia families and apparently settle any territorial disputes privately. The performances are a shakedown for money, and the hijra won't stop swaying and blessing until enough rupees have been ponied up. If you don't pay, they threaten to remove their saris (but not makeup) and dance naked. Everyone pays.

In 2009, homosexuality was decriminalized in India, much to the chagrin of Muslim clerics and Catholic clergymen. Funnily enough, lesbians were rarely prosecuted under the 148-year-old law. Every once in a while it actually pays to be overlooked by society. With regard to being gay in India today, it's pretty much the same as in America. You don't worry about walking hand in hand with your partner or kissing in public in San Francisco or Chicago, but you might think twice about it in Alabama (where studies shows that 44 percent of gays are assaulted by *their own families*).

A recent PBS documentary praised the caste system because "everyone knows their place." It seems to me that the caste system is wrong. As Sam Harris argues in his book *The Moral Landscape*, you can't excuse certain traditions as part of the culture if they have a negative impact on some individuals' well-being, like genital mutilation and the forced wearing of burkas. When you hear about today's young people being murdered for associating with partners from different castes, it's just plain barbarism.

But do we have a caste system in the United States? Those with better insurance get better healthcare. Many American Indians are living in squalor and poverty on reservations. Costly country clubs decide who is and who is not worthy of membership, just as sororities and fraternities and private clubs do on university campuses. What about legacy candidates who are accepted into top colleges because relatives went there and make healthy donations, even though the applicants' grades are below the requirements? Elite schools may offer some scholarships, but those don't exactly include allowances for yacht club couture.

Likewise, America is certainly not a country without prejudice. The last lynching was in 1981. In Mobile, Alabama, an African American named Michael Donald was strung up by two Ku Klux Klan members who kidnapped him, beat him, slit his throat, and hung him from a tree. However, many consider James Byrd Jr. to have been lynched in 1988 when two white men in Jaspar, Texas, wrapped a heavy chain around the African American man's ankles and dragged him about three miles in a pickup truck until the truck hit a gutter and Byrd's arm and head were cut off.

More recently, we had the Florida preacher who wanted to burn a copy of the Koran, Islam's holy book. President Obama, defense secretary Robert Gates, and General David Petraeus all went public to say that this was *not* a good idea for so many reasons, endangering the lives of US troops being among them. Still, the threat alone was enough to result in the torching of Christian schools in Kashmir. Six months later, the pastor carried out his Koran burning, with the upshot being that twenty-four people were killed in Afghanistan and many more injured. Such idiotic behavior at home greatly increases the chance that tourists traveling to the Middle East and North Africa will end up starring in terrorist videos prior to having their heads chopped off. And when people can no longer explore beyond their immediate horizons, cultures are bound to turn inward, away from the unfamiliar, which only exacerbates our differences.

Meantime, it might be a good idea to burn whatever high school history textbooks suggest that America is number one in everything it does. As much as I love these United States, according to a 2010 *Newsweek* study of the best countries to live in, America ranks number eleven. It didn't even make the top ten. We still have some work to do. George Bernard Shaw once described patriotism as "the conviction that a particular country is superior to all others because you were born in it."

Finally, as with most types of social progress, change tends to happen over time. A number of Indian matrimonial ads say that caste doesn't matter. This may mean that caste doesn't matter, or it may mean that a person of low caste is looking for a spouse. On the bright side, I was told by a number of parents currently seeking mates for their children that if the potential partner is educated and has a good job, then caste really isn't an issue.

Boldface Names

Mohandas Karamchand Gandhi (1869–1948). The main thing is to remember where the *H* goes in Gandhi. My aunt Sarah had her *H* floating all over the show throughout elementary school, according to her exacting older sister, a.k.a. my alleged biological mother. Gandhi, known to millions as the Mahatma, is the father figure of Indian nationalism and known for the famous quote "Be the change you wish to see in the world" (which is actually a bumper sticker version of what he really said). People are often surprised to discover that Gandhi, who was from an upper-caste family, didn't start his career as a yogi, but rather as a University of London–trained lawyer.

Gandhi entered into an arranged marriage with Kasturbai Makanji (later known as Kasturba) in a traditional Hindu wedding ceremony, when he was thirteen and she was fourteen, which was not unusual for the time. When Gandhi was fifteen, they had their first son, who died, and they went on to have four more sons who would survive to adulthood. Gandhi renounced sexual relations with his wife when he was thirty-six without giving her a choice in the matter, nor, it would appear, the option to go elsewhere.

Gandhi had a stormy relationship with his oldest son, Harilal. He wouldn't allow his son to accept a scholarship to study law in London, so the boy ran away and became an alcoholic embezzler whom Gandhi ultimately disowned. When his second son, Manilal, was caught in a cuddle with a young married Indian woman, Gandhi talked her into shaving her head and convinced Manilal to accept a lifelong vow of chastity. The three children he later fathered with his wife Sushila suggest that the pledge didn't hold. A 2007 movie titled *Gandhi, My Father* shows a slightly darker daddy dearest side to the man depicted in schoolbooks around the world as a dearly beloved leader and caused considerable controversy when it was released in India. However, members of the family, such as great-grandson Tushar Gandhi, who called it "deeply moving and very finely balanced," approved of the film. At the end of the day, it must be difficult to have a world-famous father whose time and attention is in demand by so many others. Franklin Delano Roosevelt comes to mind, who was elected to four terms as president of the United States, while his six offspring led tumultuous lives.

The politically savvy Gandhi introduced large-scale satyagraha, resistance to tyranny through mass nonviolent protests. He paved the road to independence by organizing nationwide campaigns to assist farmers and urban laborers, fight poverty, end discrimination against untouchables, improve the position of women (Gandhi favored permitting widows to remarry and the abolition of child marriage), and spearheading non-cooperation campaigns against the British. Reverend Martin Luther King Jr. was influenced by Gandhi, as evidenced by his calls for peaceful marches and sit-ins. (Fun fact: Martin Luther King Jr. was born Michael King Jr. and his father changed *both* their names.) Interestingly, Gandhi's reading of American author and tax resistor Henry David Thoreau's essay *Civil Disobedience* had reinforced his ideas about refusing to obey laws that were discriminatory through nonviolent forms of resistance and protest. Going back one step further, Thoreau had read the Eastern philosophical Hindu works Bhagavad Gita and the Upanishads.

South Africa's Nelson Mandela would similarly find inspiration in both Gandhi and King as he called for boycotts and nonviolent protests to end oppression by a white minority. Gandhi was actually working as a lawyer in South Africa when he started his life as an activist by protesting government discrimination against Indians who were living there. His faith in nonviolence was so complete that he believed women being raped should not fight their attackers but defeat them through submission and silence, and that European Jews should employ passive resistance against Hitler.

The Mahatma preached and practiced self-discipline and celibacy and frequently fasted. He concluded that by avoiding desire he was not abolishing it, so he allowed physical contact with women and in that way supposedly conquered his urges. However, insiders were shocked to discover that Gandhi was occasionally found lying naked in bed with a young woman, also unclothed and sometimes related, such as Manu, his eighteen-year-old grandniece, or else Abha, the wife of his grandnephew. These situations were always chaste, according to Gandhi.

As Gandhi was about to address a prayer meeting on January 30, 1948, just six months after Indian independence, he was shot to death by Hindu nationalist Nathuram Godse. Hindu extremists were angry at Gandhi because he'd finally agreed to Partition (even though it was by then a fait accompli) and because he advocated peace with the Muslims (or "appeasement of Muslims," in the words of his assassin). Brutality was being rained down upon Hindus in Pakistan and Kashmir (likewise, there was violence toward Muslims by Hindus in India), and Hindu separatists wanted to knock the Muslims back into the eighth century without interference from the Mahatma.

When Gandhi first began campaigning against British rule, they looked upon him with amusement. Two decades later, they regarded him as a brilliant leader, consummate politician, and the greatest threat to their continued dominance of the subcontinent. However, some modern historians argue that the British were prepared to relinquish India by the 1940s, and Gandhi's fierce stand for independence didn't play much of a role in the decision.

Modern-day Indian journalists and historians often give Gandhi a mixed report card. There is criticism about how he handled Partition and also of his rural romanticism. Gandhi mandated that village life be India's soul, along with simplicity and humility, thus he wasn't a proponent of industrialization, modernization, technology, or even constitutional democracy. Railroads, telegraphs, foreign goods, lawyers, doctors, hospitals, and birth control all had to go, as far as the Mahatma was concerned. "If there were no hospitals for venereal diseases or even for consumptives, we would have less consumption, and less sexual vice amongst us." (The fickle finger of fate has made the country home to several Gandhi Hospitals and the Gandhi Medical College.) Nevertheless, Indians, like most people, turned out to have a predilection for healthcare and consumerism. Furthermore, a philosophy of nonviolence isn't exactly tenable in a nuclear nation whose military is regularly called upon to address border disputes. Meantime, kids without video games and texting? Forget it.

Still, Indians continue to be sensitive about Gandhi's reputation, and as recently as 2011, the government of Gandhi's home state of Gujarat banned the book *Great Soul* by former *New York Times* editor and Pulitzer Prize-winner Joseph Lelyveld for discussing a close friendship Gandhi had with a German man who was probably a homosexual. I'm not sure how book banning squares with democracy, but I guess it's better than issuing a fatwa (Islamic death sentence) like the one that landed on Indian-born writer Salman Rushdie's head after publishing *The Satanic Verses*, compliments of Iran's Ayatollah Khomeini. No matter, an irreverent depiction of sacred leaders is still the fastest and cheapest way to create a best seller.

Finally, I find it odd that Gandhi was never awarded the Nobel Peace Prize. Especially when you consider that during the same period, one went to US secretary of state Cordell Hull (in 1945), who advised President Roosevelt to send back to Europe the SS *St. Louis*, which carried 936 asylum-seeking Jews, most of whom were later killed in the Holocaust. One of Gandhi's greatest contributions to political activism, which we've recently seen used to enormous effect across the Middle East and the Occupy Wall Street movement in the United States, is the practice of bringing together large numbers of highly motivated and disciplined protesters in public places. The white loincloth as spiritual statement may not have withstood the test of time, but he certainly succeeded in utilizing the collective power of moral authority, especially when spotlighted by international media. At the Gandhi museum in Ahmadabad, this is one of his many quotes featured: "The Seven Deadly Sins are wealth without work, pleasure without conscience, knowledge without character, business without morality, science without humanity, worship without sacrifice, and politics without principle." And that alone was worth the price of admission.

Sarojini Naidu (1879–1949) was a poet and freedom fighter also known as The Nightingale of India. A fierce activist in the Independence movement, she also lectured around the country on child welfare, fair labor practices, Hindu-Muslim unity and women's rights. During one campaign for home rule, she was jailed for twenty-one months along with Gandhi. They became close friends, and apparently the Mahatma didn't mind Naidu calling him Mickey Mouse. Naidu knew that Gandhi's ashram compound on the banks of the Sabarmati River, where it was forbidden to kill even snakes, didn't generate enough income to stay solvent and therefore required financing by Ahmadabad textile magnates and Bombay shipping barons, which gave rise to her most famous quip: "It took a lot of money to keep him in poverty." Naidu also said, "When there is oppression, the only self-respecting thing is to rise and say this shall cease today." She was so concerned about the world's downtrodden that she even managed a trip to New York in 1928 to call attention to the plight of Native Americans and African Americans. Naidu was the first woman to become president of the Indian National Congress and the governor of an Indian state. Her immensely popular poetry celebrated contemporary Indian life and featured beggars, fishermen, widows, peddlers, milkmaids, dancers, and rickshaw drivers.

Jawaharlal Nehru (1889–1964). This is not a Spanish dude, and so, yes, you pronounce the *J*. Nehru was an Indian statesman and the first prime minister of an independent India, from 1947 until his death, in 1964. Nehru and his politically active father, Motilal Nehru, along with Mahatma Gandhi, were sometimes referred to as the Father, Son, and Holy Ghost. Nehru worked closely with Britain's Lord Mountbatten during the transition to home rule, and most believe that Lady Mountbatten and the widowed Nehru were in the throes of a passionate love affair. Even Lady Mountbatten's own children later admitted that she was a hard gal to keep on the verandah. Nehru was a student of history, nuanced thinker, talented strategist, and truly deserving of his title the Architect of Modern India. He brought democracy, secularism, and socialism to a society built on regionalism, tribalism, and religion. Nehru even went so far as to ensure that the constitution granted some basic rights to women.

Nehru clearly had his sights set on becoming the first prime minister during the lead-up to Independence. But when Gandhi saw that there was a bad moon on the rise with regard to the Muslims wanting to break off and form Pakistan, the clever peacemaker suggested that Nehru allow Mohammed Ali Jinnah, leader of the Muslims, to become the first prime minister of a united India to demonstrate that Hindus and Muslims could live side by side in harmony. Although Jinnah tried to keep it a secret, Gandhi and Nehru knew that he suffered from tuberculosis and lung cancer and would not be in charge of anything for long, so Nehru would soon have his chance. Jinnah smoked like a chimney and was rarely far from a bottle of whiskey, and there are those who say he even ate ham sandwiches, all of which happen to be on most Muslims' list of Things Not To Do. Besides that, he didn't favor traditional Muslim dress, rarely entered a mosque, spoke little Urdu, and couldn't recite from the Koran. Nevertheless, Nehru wanted to be the first prime minister rather than the second prime minister and so the offer, which, had it been accepted, might have prevented the bloodshed of more than a million people following Partition, was never made. And if it had been made, Jinnah, by then in favor of starting his own Muslim democracy, would most likely have rejected the proposal. Consequently, Jinnah became the first governor-general of Pakistan, on August 15,

1947, and did indeed die just over a year later, on September 11, 1948.

Jawaharlal Nehru went on to become India's longest-serving prime minister to date and spawned a dynasty, with his daughter and grandson becoming prime ministers and his great-grandson currently next in line. Despite being raised in a Hindu family, Nehru was an atheist who went so far as to write, "Religion as practiced in India has become the old man of the sea for us and it has not only broken our backs but stifled and almost killed all originality of thought or mind." For this reason, he'd specifically requested not to have a Hindu funeral. However, his politically astute daughter thought otherwise and gave him a traditional Hindu wake, followed by cremation on a funeral pyre lit by his grandson.

You're not truly international until a drink, like a Bloody Mary or Earl Grey tea, or a garment, such as the Che beret or the bright red Garibaldi shirt, is named after you. The unisex hip-length tailored jacket with a round stand-up collar favored by India's first prime minister is to this day known as a Nehru jacket.

Fun fact: Gandhi, Jinnah, and Nehru were all born in India but trained as lawyers in England.

Indira Gandhi (1917–1984). Isn't she Mahatma Gandhi's daughter or granddaughter? No. Indira Priyadarshini Nehru was the only daughter of Jawaharlal

Nehru and his wife, Kamala. The man who married Indira was a Parsi, born Feroze Gandhy, but during the late 1930s began to spell his last name as Gandhi. At least that's the official version. Any Indian will happily tell you how this is all a big cover-up because Feroze was born a Muslim with the family name of Khan, and it was plain to see that Indira would not have a political future with such a husband. So Feroze supposedly asked Mahatma Gandhi to approve this love match, which hadn't been arranged by their parents and, in fact, was generally frowned upon. Gandhi ostensibly agreed and adopted Feroze so that the young suitor could change his name to Gandhi.

Indira Ghandi, who first took the reins as prime minister in 1966, would become one of the most powerful women in the world, which seems paradoxical in a country that was known for subjugating women. Indira claimed that she did not fancy herself a feminist and frequently extolled the virtues of being a mother and homemaker. Yet she referred to women as "the biggest oppressed minority in the world" and said that Indian women were handicapped from birth.

Interestingly, there's a tradition of dynastic politics in South Asia where women often rise to prominence as the daughters or wives of powerful men, many of whom have been assassinated or else the victims of violence. Pakistan's eleventh prime minister, Benazir Bhutto, inherited the political mantle of her father,

Prime Minister Zulfikar Ali Bhutto, who was over-thrown in 1977 and executed two years later. (Benazir would be assassinated while campaigning in 2007.) In Sri Lanka, Sirimavo Bandaranaike rose to power after the assassination of her husband, W. R. D. Bandara-naike, in 1959. And in Bangladesh, for a time the two most prominent opposition leaders were the daughter and widow of assassinated former presidents. How-ever, the nepotism reality show prize goes to the South Indian state of Tamil Nadu, where the 1987 death of chief minister and former film star M. G. Ramachan-dran sparked waves of looting and rioting across the entire state that lasted for a month. Ramchandran's wife and mistress both fought publicly to succeed him. His wife of twenty-four years triumphed over his mis-tress (who preferred to be called a "protégée"), but that didn't last long and they ended up forming a coali-tion in 1988. Corazon Aquino was the first woman president of the Philippines (1986–1992) and despite being a self-proclaimed "plain housewife," had been married to the popular Senator Benigno Aquino Jr., who was assassinated in 1983. (BTW, Aquino is not the shoe lady—that was Imelda, widow of former Philippine president Ferdinand Marcos.) The first female president of Indonesia (2001–2004), Megawati Sukarnoputri, just happened to be the daughter of the country's first president, Sukarno. And in August 2011, Yingluck Shinawatra was sworn in as the first female prime minister of Thailand. Coincidentally, her brother, ex-prime minister Thaksin Shinawatra, lives in exile after having been overthrown in a 2006 military coup while facing charges of authoritarianism and corruption. (The Supreme Court later found him guilty of abnormal wealth and seized $232 million of his frozen assets.)

Indira Gandhi went on to be elected prime minister four times and dominated the subcontinent for almost two decades. The period was not without controversy, particularly when she suspended democracy for twenty-one months between 1975 and 1977.

In June of 1984, Indira Gandhi ordered Operation Bluestar, in which Indian military was used to remove Sikh separatists (they wanted a Sikh homeland in the Punjab area) from the previously mentioned Golden Temple in Amritsar, where they were amassing weapons. Government-generated reports claimed that 83 soldiers died along with 492 civilians, although independent estimates put the number as high as 8,000. As a result, the operation was highly controversial. Four months later, on October 31, 1984, Indira Gandhi was assassinated by two of her Sikh bodyguards. Following that, more than 5,000 Sikhs were killed in anti-Sikh rioting.

Indira's son Rajiv Gandhi served as prime minister from his mother's death until his defeat in 1989. On May 21, 1991, while out campaigning for a party member, he was killed by a female suicide bomber, along with fourteen others. The attack was meant as vengeance by a group of separatist guerillas in Sri Lanka, where Rajiv had sent a peacekeeping force while prime minister.

Indira's second son, Sanjay Gandhi, was also involved in politics, and has been criticized for his role in a family planning program that involved the forced sterilization of hundreds of thousands men and women. Sanjay crashed a plane that he was flying, killing himself and the only passenger.

Rahul Gandhi is the great-grandson of India's first prime minister, the grandson of India's fourth prime minister, and the son of India's seventh prime minister. His mother is Italian-born Sonia Gandhi, the widow of Indira's eldest son, Rajiv, and a powerful behind-the-scenes political player. Stay tuned, as there seems to be all the tabloid drama of the Kennedy family in this dynastic saga. A miniseries is surely in the making.

Jiddu Krishnamurti (1895–1986). J-Krish or K-murti, as the media would no doubt dub him today, was India's first great secular guru. Though born into a Hindu Brahman family, this philosopher believed that the path to truth, self-improvement, life without conflict, and problem solving was open to everyone, and that "Religion is the frozen thought of man out of which they build temples." Actually, Krishnamurti might best be called the antiguru since he also denounced the concept of saviors and spiritual leaders. Yet he claimed to have psychic experiences in which he talked to his dead sister and mother. Since the author and philosopher seems to contradict himself on occasion, below are a few Krishnamurtisms so he can speak for himself.

> Hitler and Mussolini were only the primary spokesmen for the attitude of domination and craving for power that are in the heart of almost everyone. Until the source is cleared, there will always be confusion and hate, wars and class antagonisms.

> You must understand the whole of life, not just one little part of it. That is why you must read, that is why you must look at the skies, that is why you must sing and dance, and write poems and suffer and understand, for all that is life.

> Violence is not merely killing another. It is violence when we use a sharp word, when we make a gesture to brush away a person, when we obey because there is fear. So violence isn't merely organized butchery in the name of God, in the name of society or country. Violence is much more subtle, much deeper, and we are inquiring into the very depths of violence.

At this point, you're probably thinking that the name Krishna sounds mighty familiar. In accordance with common Hindu practice, as an eighth child who happened to be male, Jiddu (Jiddu was the family name) Krishnamurti was named after the Hindu god Krishna. Krishna, often depicted as a young boy playing the flute, is viewed through a kaleidoscope of possibilities—divine hero, god-child, prankster, lover, and supreme being. Just as Hindus have thousands of deities, each one can have various interpretations. So if any Catholic was thinking that there are an awful lot of saints to keep up with, be glad you're not in charge of putting together a compendium called *The Lives of the Gods* in India.

Monkeys and Tigers
and Snakes, Oh My!

Despite environmental challenges caused by the demands of such an enormous population, India is teeming with wildlife, much of which can be viewed in the country's hundreds of national parks. However, many of the animals are unaware of such parks and happily dwell in the countryside, suburbs, and cities, much like prairie dogs in Lubbock, Texas, who are ignorant of the fact that an entire homeland was set up expressly for them by generous (eccentric?) benefactor Kennedy N. Clapp, who was then named mayor of Prairie Dog Town in perpetuity. Other species are being pushed out of their natural habitats by the rapid pace of development.

Monkeys are so prevalent that they're fighting each other over limited turf and resources. In New Delhi, langur monkeys have chased red-brown rhesus monkeys out of the grand government buildings that flank the Presidential Palace, and it's become a regular *West Side Story* of rival primate gangs duking it out, retitled the Monkey Menace by locals. However, the langurs have cleverly gotten humans on their side, and during the 2010 Commonwealth Games, they were deployed to patrol stadiums and the athletes' village and scare off other smaller monkeys along with the occasional cobra.

When not snatching unguarded food, monkeys will climb into open-air dining rooms and filch jam pots and bread baskets or whatever else they can get their prehensile tails around. One clever monkey entered a hotel room through a second-story balcony door and stole a woman's hormone replacement therapy drugs. Little did Mr. Monkey know that he was volunteering to participate in a scientific experiment.

Otherwise, there's been monkey business at the highest levels of government. In 2004, monkeys threatened India's national security by scattering top-secret documents around a Ministry of Defense office. And in 2007, Delhi's deputy mayor S. S. Bajwa died as a result of serious head injuries after falling from his first-floor terrace while attempting to fight off a pack of wild monkeys.

However, monkey culling isn't possible, because they're considered sacred by devout Hindus, who view them as a manifestation of the monkey god Hanuman. He's worshipped by villagers as a protective guardian, by ascetics as a yogi, and by wrestlers and body builders for his power and strength. To give you an idea of Hanuman's importance, his Wikipedia entry is the same length as that of Lady Gaga, Elton John, and most American presidents. And instead of saying that someone has Attention Deficit Disorder, Indians describe this condition as Mad Monkey Mind.

Rats, on the other hand, are not sacred, and the mayors of large cities hire professional rat killers. India is home to the gray-black bandicoot, which is the largest species of rat in the world, aside from the towering thirty-foot-high inflatable rat with buckteeth and beady eyes seen at US worksites protesting the hiring of nonunion labor. Bandicoot rats can be more than a foot in length, have the ability to decimate entire crops of wheat and grain in short order, and emit a piglike grunt when attacking. As a group, bandicoot rats are capable of killing and devouring a human child.

When people say the Big Four in the United States, they're almost always referring to the major accounting firms, occasionally the four most-popular heavy metal bands, and every once in awhile the Allied leaders who met at the Paris Peace Conference in 1919. India's Big Four are venomous snakes: Russell's viper, Indian cobra, common krait, and the saw-scaled viper. They all feed on rodents, so you'll find them where there are plenty of rats, which is where there also tend to be a lot of people, since rats thrive on garbage produced by humans. Most bites occur by stepping on a snake at night. However, there is a serum widely available, much the way breath mints and bullets are in the States.

The king cobra, which famously starred as an evildoer in Rudyard Kipling's short story "Rikki-Tikki-Tavi" and continues to hog all the good movie roles, is the largest venomous snake in the world. A king cobra bite can kill a person in fifteen minutes and a full-grown elephant in a few hours. However, the king prefers to live in dense jungles, where it can feed on other snakes, so you don't usually hear about them having adventures with humans, unless an Agatha Christie or Sherlock Holmes story is being filmed.

Attention, ophidiophobes. Serpents do not lurk around every corner or hide under hotel beds. I did not see a single free-ranging reptile throughout my trip, which included animal sanctuaries and national parks. So it'd be silly for someone to skip India for fear of running into a snake, since they're everywhere throughout the United States. In New York State alone we have three types of poisonous snakes—rattlers, copperheads, and massasauga—along with seriously scary-looking milk snakes, water snakes, and eight-foot black rat snakes. Nonetheless, during a childhood spent largely out of doors, I managed not to become a meal for a single one of them. Yes, vipers live among us, and we among them.

Snake charming is a dying profession in India, largely a result of the 1972 Wildlife Protection Act, which prohibits owning and selling serpents but wasn't really enforced until animal-rights activists became involved during the 1990s. However, you can occasionally find practitioners of this ancient art at marketplaces, tourist attractions, and festivals, hypnotizing snakes by playing musical instruments and sometimes handling the snakes. Snakes are considered to be sacred, and their charmers are regarded as holy men who are influenced by the gods. Ancient artwork regularly depicts the various gods being guarded by cobras. Most snake charmers (at least the ones still living) have removed the poison glands from the snake's head or defanged it. Spoiler alert: snakes don't really dance to the music since they have very poor hearing (do you see any ears?), but they can sense vibrations along the ground. The snake may also sway in an effort to defend itself against a charmer's hand or flute moving above its head.

While American presidents have been known to travel with mountain bikes, golf pros, and decks of cards, Indian presidents always head to the summer retreat with at least four snake wranglers and one monkey catcher. In 2000 (the last year for which figures are available), a total of four snakes managed to sneak into the executive retreat. At least guests needn't fret that the proverbial bump in the night is a restless ghost.

As India's building boom continues, many former snake charmers are re-careering as snake rescuers, capturing snakes everywhere from presidential palaces to suburban homes and returning them to the wild. I can only hope this works better than my dad's effort to relocate the bird-feeder-raiding squirrels in his yard to the dam site five miles away, as it seems to take them less than a day to make the journey back home.

Not surprisingly, India's infamously apathetic bureaucracy has even aggravated the snake-charming community. A man from the northern state of Uttar Pradesh who had saved many lives over the years by gallantly removing poisonous snakes that were interacting with the citizenry was fed up with a local government that had for years delayed the issuance of a plot of land where he could conserve his snakes, despite it having been approved by senior authorities. So, as an incentive to complete the process, Mr. Hakkul unleashed his vipers in the land revenues office building. The result was that employees quickly cleared out on their own accord and within minutes the snakes had their sanctuary. Perhaps this will go down in Indian history as "pulling a Hakkul."

A hundred years ago, there were more than forty-five thousand tigers roaming India, and now there are only about seventeen hundred. The Brits fancied themselves the Great White Hunters and did a good job at decimating the Bengal tiger population. Otherwise, poaching, deforestation, mining, insecticides, and industrial development continue to have a negative impact on the big cats. Strong demand for tiger skins in China and Tibet is still a serious problem when it comes to preservation. Add in the fact that tiger bones, teeth, and nails are used in traditional Chinese medicine (to treat ailments such as arthritis) and they've just about run through their own supply of South China tigers. The year 2010 was the Year of the Tiger in China, but instead of raising awareness about conservation, it only served to drive up demand for tiger skins and parts. More than forty reserves around the subcontinent are in operation to protect the Bengal tiger, but even such guarded sanctuaries fall victim to poachers. Demand is so high that hunters are willing to go to great lengths and take enormous risks to kill these animals. Meantime, India remains a key player in preservation, since it is home to about half of all the world's wild tigers. Much like game parks that allow you to enjoy wildlife in Africa, tourist dollars spent on seeing the tigers in their habitats help save them from extinction in the wild.

I say "in the wild," because tigers, unlike pandas, breed extremely well in captivity. The United States alone has an estimated forty-five thousand tigers in expected places like zoos and preserves, and unexpected places such as New York City apartments, New Jersey backyards, and Minnesota basements. On the plus side, I haven't heard of any prowling the sewers, yet. You can buy tiger cubs on the Internet for between five hundred and two thousand dollars, but I wouldn't recommend it since within a year they'll need twenty pounds of fresh meat per day and stalk any other pets you own, and most have a habit of swiping and biting, which leads to surgery and skin grafts.

Did you know that if you shave a tiger, it has striped skin underneath? Not that I'm suggesting you try it.

Game Changers: Women and Children

Historical research suggests that during ancient times, Indian women enjoyed equal status with men in almost all walks of life. They married at a mature age and were free to select their own spouses and could even work in the ESP arts as highly revered sages and seers. However, that all took a major dive in the Middle Ages with the adoption of child marriage, polygamy, women having to cover themselves and sometimes live in restricted areas, the practice of wives committing suicide upon their husband's demise, and, for those who didn't, a ban on widows remarrying. Despite being in a region of the world where many of these medieval practices are still in place, India's women are clearly heading for modernity. They've taken places in all the skilled professions and also as CEOs, prime minister, president, state governors, speaker of the Lok Sabha, leader of the Opposition, and president of the Indian National Congress, one of the two major political parties. And if that's not proof enough, there have been more than two dozen Mumbai Mafia queens.

Still, change happens slowly, especially in such a large country with diverse traditions. Despite more than a decade of high economic growth and expanding upper and middle classes, more than 40 percent of Indians live below the World Bank poverty line of $1.25 a day. Close to half of all children under the age of three are malnourished, and India has the highest rate of child labor in the world. At least 50 million school-age children are working in agriculture, as house servants, rolling cheap cigarettes, weaving carpets, or as prostitutes. As a result, India has one of the worst literacy rates, especially for girls, where 47 percent of the female population lack an education and cannot even read or write. It doesn't help that about half of all Indian women are married off before the legal age of eighteen. In villages, girls are sometimes married before they reach the age of ten. Is anyone else thinking AMBER Alert?

People cite the success of Indian marriages because of the low divorce rate. Well, the divorce rate in the States was much lower when women could be turned out with no money or property or social status and in some cases even lost legal control of their children. In most countries there's a direct correlation between the prevalence of divorce and the stigma and financial penalty that results from divorce.

Proponents of arranged marriages like to insist that these are by and large happier than love matches.

I'm not going to pick a fight with arranged marriage, which still accounts for about 90 percent of all nuptials, so long as it's the modern style where the victims, I mean young people, have the right to veto potential partners. In my opinion, an arranged marriage doesn't seem all that different from typing your dreams and hobbies into an Internet dating service. The joke about courting Indian-style is that your first date consists of meeting the parents, your second date is to agree on the wedding, and your third date is the wedding night.

However, newspaper and online advertisements for "incredibly beautiful" brides and "extremely handsome" grooms never fail to amuse with their outsized desperation for doctors, emphasis on light skin, requests for horoscopes, and occasional caste requirements. Although, when a high-paying international job or medical degree is in play, a number of other prerequisites can apparently be overlooked. It stands to reason that people want to portray themselves in the best light possible, and therefore you'll also find ads for matrimonial detectives who specialize in marriage fraud to ferret out who might be lying. For a little extra, they'll provide you with an additional dossier on your future mother-in-law.

Indian mothers-in-law are of course renowned for being the butt of jokes and as instigators of the many wicked machinations (which mostly involve torturing daughters-in-law) that drive soap opera story lines.

Perhaps afraid of losing their power as a result of new measures that favor daughters-in-law claiming abuse, groups such as the All India Mother-in-law Protection Forum are popping up so this increasingly put-upon faction can exchange grievances and compare remedies (and perhaps exchange wily tactics and nefarious schemes). Even if more young women become professionals, arranged marriage goes by the wayside, and social security starts taking care of the old, don't count those evil mothers-in-law out just yet. Every mother-in-law was once a daughter-in-law, so there are untold scores that still need to be settled.

To better understand such customs, Westerners must also recognize that living in extended families is a long-standing part of the culture. Many Indians will happily inform you that Americans raise children the way animals raise their young, caring for them just until they're old enough to make a living and then tossing them out on their own, into the cold and cruel wilderness of society at large.

One thing you don't see in the matrimonial ads are references to sports prowess. Despite being extremely talented at the game of cricket, Indians appear not to have distinguished themselves in many other areas of athleticism and are routinely criticized for leaving the Olympics with few medals in hand, particularly since they have access to more than a billion potentially gifted athletes. Furthermore, I saw countless impossibly skinny men darting through crowded streets pulling carts and rickshaws loaded with ten times the drivers' weight in people and metal pipes, so there's certainly no lack of coordination, strength, determination, or dexterity among the populace. I'm venturing a guess that Indians aren't diving into cold swimming pools or sharpening speed skates at dawn because they're busy prepping for MCATs. Sticking the landing on a perfect balance beam routine may get you a gold medal, but an MD after your name is apparently what lands a gold wedding band around here.

One problem with marriage in India today is that many require a (potentially large) dowry be paid by the bride's family to the groom's family. What happened to the African system where the *groom* had to pay a couple of cows to the *bride's family* for the pleasure of her company? I mean, the bride is expected to go to the house of her Indian husband and cook and clean and take care of everyone, including his parents. The only thing making her life easier is that Indian children are not taught to walk, talk, or use the toilet. As in African tribes and large Irish Catholic families, they pick it up from the other kids, like cursing and knowledge about sex.

Such as it is, a number of men are experiencing dowry remorse, and after agreeing on an amount, they soon decide it's not enough and then want a flat-screen TV. This and the failure to produce a son can result in harm to women. It often takes the form of a horrendous cooking "accident," known as bride burning, which is a subset of dowry death, where murdering your wife is passed off as suicide or an accident, which is a subset of violence toward women. Much the way Bangalore is known for information technology and Goa is famous for its beaches, the northwest state of Rajasthan would appear to be the cooking accident capital of the world.

Unfortunately, this tradition is on the rise, with more than eight thousand recorded cases per year, which is up 50 percent from a decade ago, and many go unreported. The low survival rate keeps these crimes from being prosecuted, and of those that are prosecuted, few convictions result. Cases move through the courts slowly to allow plenty of time for the accused to bribe officials. Like *Jarndyce v. Jarndyce* in the Charles Dickens novel *Bleak House*, the long wait for a court date occasionally outlasts the litigants. Men accused of bride burning can easily remarry, while the women who manage to survive, about 10 percent, are considered damaged goods and for the most part cannot. The sad fact is that many more women are killed in bride burnings in democratic India than in honor killings throughout the Muslim world.

As a result of demands by women's rights activists, the Indian government has changed inheritance laws and permitted daughters to claim equal rights to their parental property so they're not entirely dependent on their husband and in-laws. Women who control money and property are less likely to become victims of domestic violence. People are also being encouraged to rein in the tradition of spending so lavishly on weddings.

Otherwise, one bizarre custom appears to be on the way out entirely. The Hindu tradition of suttee is where a perfectly healthy wife climbs atop the funeral pyre of her dead husband as an expression of her (undying?) love for him. Suttee began to disappear after the British banned the practice in 1829, but in Rajasthan it still occurs in some of the more distant villages, with about fifty cases thought to have taken place since Independence. The government is firmly against suttee and not only denounces the archaic practice but treats it as a criminal offense. The problem is that despite having been outlawed, suttee is still glorified to some extent by dint of people worshipping the site where it occurred, elevating the victim to a goddess, and professing admiration for her courage. Talk about mixed messages. As it happens, one can see how suttee was considered the better alternative for a widow than to face a life of abuse from in-laws who frequently blamed the daughter-in-law for her husband's death or forced her to beg in the streets.

The Elements trilogy is a series of films dealing with social reform by Indian-born Canadian film director and screenwriter Deepa Mehta. Her Academy Award-nominated *Water* (2005) is about a married child who becomes a widow in 1938 and after having her hair shorn and jewelry removed is dumped at an ashram that forces young women into prostitution to cover the group's living expenses. (In the first few minutes, you can see the aforementioned swastikas.) The young but perceptive child asks, "Where is the house for men widows?" And of course there isn't one, just as there were never homes for unwed fathers in the West. *Fire* (1996) deals with the issues of homosexuality and arranged marriage in patriarchal India, and *Earth* (1998) centers on the religious strife associated with the creation of Pakistan. All three movies have caused controversy, but *Fire* and *Water* received particularly heavy criticism from conservatives who viewed them as attacks on Hindu culture. After *Fire* was released, Mehta required twenty-four-hour police protection for almost a year. The struggle to make *Water* is depicted in the nonfiction book *Shooting Water: A Mother-Daughter Journey and the Making of the Film*, written by Mehta's daughter, Devyani Saltzman.

Indian women gained the right to abortion in 1971 without a battle, a year and half before *Roe v. Wade* made it legal in the United States. However, the subcontinent still maintains a high birthrate, despite thousands of unnecessary deaths due to the lack of access to medical care and a fear that it's bad luck to give birth outside of the home. India has the highest rate of maternal deaths in the world, with seventy-eight thousand women dying every year during pregnancy, childbirth, or within forty-two days of delivery, of which 75 percent would've been preventable with some rudimentary fixes. The old Sanskrit saying "May you be the mother of a hundred sons" can seem more of a curse than a blessing. Such enormous value put on the birth of males over females results in not only infanticide but also the neglect of girls when it comes to nutrition, immunization, and education. In rural areas, a female child is often suffocated or poisoned, while wealthier people will have an abortion following sex determination, even though sex testing is supposedly illegal. Still, 914 girls are born for every 1,000 boys and the gap is expanding. In 2011, a man who was employed as a leather worker took his two daughters, ages two and three, and drowned them in a village well, while sparing his four-month-old son. He later told police that he couldn't afford to keep the girls.

In India, the death rate among female children allowed to live tends to be higher, despite a biological tendency to be stronger at birth than boys. In other words, infanticide is occurring because girls are less desirable than boys. A daughter can't take over the family business because she must be given away in marriage to another family. Marrying her off will be enormously expensive, whereas a boy will one day bring home a dowry, which will increase the finances of the entire family since sons are supposed to care for their parents in old age. Also, according to Hindu tradition, a son is necessary to light his parents' funeral pyres.

Meantime, women are often treated poorly after giving birth to girls, especially if they haven't yet had a son. Someone needs to remind their husbands that it is the man who determines the sex of a child.

Surely you've heard a version of the quote "Ginger Rogers did everything that Fred Astaire did, except in high heels and backward." Proportionally, more women work in India than in any other country, despite having more children than women in most other countries. Women can be found in almost every type of job, including construction, road building, farming, and mining, even at the lowest levels. They often keep up a full schedule while pregnant or breast-feeding and go home to cook, clean, and take care of elderly parents.

Furthermore, the current level of rape is high but impossible to quantify, since most go unreported due to the stigma associated with being subjected to this hideous act. If women would start reporting rapes, then incidence would drop swiftly, since men currently feel they can attack with impunity as almost no victim wants the world to know that "her honor has been destroyed." Obviously, educated and supportive families and communities are also necessary to bring this particular change about. Women shouldn't be made to feel ashamed for being assaulted.

The situation of women and children (especially

girls) clearly has much room for improvement, but before examining some solutions, it's a good idea to remember that there's plenty of violence against women in the United States including rape, and there are people who believe that a woman who is the victim of rape and incest should be forced to carry the child to term.

Women's groups in India are busy advocating for reform and educating people as I write this. The birth rate is currently 2.6 children, way down from twenty years ago. One sterilization campaign offering cash prizes became so popular that a number of men went back two and three times. However, my favorite program has to be the short-lived 2008 offer of guns in return for vasectomies, so a man wouldn't be left shooting blanks. Some states currently offer monetary incentives of about a hundred dollars for newly married couples to delay starting a family by a few years.

As always, it's not just about changing laws but also expectations and traditions, which takes time and diligence. This will have to be part of a concerted campaign against bride burnings, infanticide, and other forms of violence against women, such as depriving them of healthcare and proper nutrition. Here are some ideas for change that deserve our support and encouragement:

1) Abolish dowries. In many countries, people pay for a bride. Let's just split the difference and no cash changes hands.

2) Stop marrying off young people. The law says that males must be twenty-one and girls must be eighteen, but this isn't enforced, and couples much younger still marry, especially in rural areas. And what's the joke with the age differential for males and females?

3) Provide social security so old people aren't dependent on children, especially daughters-in-law.

4) Reform healthcare. Every year, there are 2 million new cases of tuberculosis, an easily eradicable disease, which is the leading cause of death among people between fifteen and forty-five, the core of India's workforce. Public hospitals are overburdened and underequipped, leaving 80 percent of medical services in private hands, and it's common for "doctors" and "technicians" not to have any medical training at all. Healthcare costs are the most prevalent cause of personal bankruptcy. Despite India's emergence as a top destination for medical tourism, when Sonia Gandhi required treatment in 2011, she traveled to the United States.

5) Organize, computerize, supervise, and deputize. Free and discounted rations (similar to

our food stamps) tend not to make it to their destination as a result of corruption, bureaucratic bungling, or because people aren't aware of their entitlement.

6) Lose the expectation that women be virgins when married. Why does this only apply to women? After all, the ancient Hindu text *Kama Sutra* recognizes that women also have sexual desires.

7) Require all children to attend school. Everyone agrees that better education for women will solve a multitude of problems. A study commissioned by the Bill and Melinda Gates Foundation showed that educating young women resulted in saving the lives of more than 4 million children worldwide in 2009. The classroom is also a great place to learn about family planning and HIV prevention. In countries with mandatory schooling, people marry later, have children later and fewer of them, and regularly begin their sentences with "My therapist says...." Smaller families place less of a burden on an already strained food and water supply. The Right to Education Act of 2010 promised schooling to every child from age six to fourteen and now it

needs to be fully implemented and enforced.

8) Extend a small monthly benefit to poor families who keep their daughters in school as an incentive to prevent girls from being sold into prostitution, put to work in fields and factories, or married off at a young age. "When you educate a boy, you educate an individual; but if you educate a girl, you educate a community," says the African proverb. Educated women have better job prospects and earning power and are therefore less likely to become victims of domestic violence. (This has been successful in a number of Indian villages.)

9) Issue birth certificates to children born outside of hospitals so they have access to government schools and services rather than spend their lives classified as undocumented, despite being born in India. (A program is currently under way to create a database of all citizens and issue identity numbers.)

10) Upgrade schools with better facilities, supplies, and more teacher accountability.

11) Offer free breakfast to schoolchildren in poor communities. (This has also been attempted in

a few places on a small scale.) Once women and girls are properly nourished, the multibillion-dollar diet industry can get a proper foothold in the country, and we'll know once and for all how many Weight Watchers points to add following a dinner of rasam, rogan josh, and gulab jamun. Spinning, Jazzercise, buttrobics classes with "I'm Too Sexy for My Sari" playing in the background, and Tasti D-Lite franchises are just around the corner.

I've heard many people say that the way women are treated in certain countries is cultural and nothing should be done about it, or, at the very least, it's none of our business. However, humans are interconnected, and I think we should care whether or not others are being treated poorly or unfairly. I first heard the following idea from Warren Buffett, but I don't believe he takes credit for it. What Buffett likes to call the Ovarian Lottery and others have termed the Luck of the Draw essentially goes like this: You're not born yet and you have to create the world that you're going to live in. The problem is, you don't know whether you're going to be male or female; white, brown, or black; blind or sighted; handicapped or not; born to a Brahman or an untouchable, a Catholic or a Muslim. If you'd be satisfied being *any* combination of these things in the world you've created, then it is indeed a wonderful world. If not, change it.

India Unbound

For decades we've been hearing that prosperity is just around the corner for the subcontinent. So where's the proof that this is finally India's moment? It's in the mouse. Disney is coming. An amusement park that will franchise Disney rides is currently in the planning stages by Bollywood mogul Manmohan Shetty. It's a small world after all.

I was just kidding about that being the sine qua non of success, but the report is nonetheless real, and it's going to require a lot of mouse ears. India is one-third the size of the United States, with four times as many people. It's the world's largest democracy with the second-largest army of any country (after China) and possesses nukes, as do neighboring Pakistan and China. A president serves as the head of state with a prime minister as head of the government and a two-house parliament that is elected by the people (the lower house directly and the upper house indirectly, through state assemblies). It's largely based on the British system, so rather than the people directly electing their leader, the president is chosen by members of

Parliament and state legislatures, and then he or she appoints the prime minister, who is the head of the majority party. Many constituents feel that they should be voting directly for their leader, the way many in the United States would like to eradicate the electoral college and simply have a one person, one vote policy.

Signs of progress are to be found almost everywhere throughout India today, from the towering skyscrapers in its big cities to the small computers that have been placed in rural homes so locals can bank long distance. Ironically, IT came late to India, particularly in government offices, banks, and the stock market, with many managers kicking and screaming against modernization and agreeing to install computers only because air conditioners came with them (so the circuitry wouldn't melt).

Nowadays, more than 750 million people have cell phones and an additional 15 million are sold every month. And while providing increased business efficiencies, they're also giving young people a new degree of freedom and privacy. Almost every person with any sort of an income carries a phone, as these devices have officially entered Maslow's hierarchy of needs, right after curry, sleep, and shelter. Heck, even die-hard Communists have cell phones, which might be considered the ultimate capitalist tool. (Did they not like the old system where a bureaucrat decided if and when you could have a phone?) Furthermore, connectivity is so comprehensive that from a tiny West Coast fishing village, I was able to call my father in the New Mexico desert and have it sound as if he was in the next room, whereas the same phone cuts out every time I take the Central Park transverse road in Manhattan. Should someone be studying the fact that al-Qaeda is running an international terrorist network from caves in the mountains of Southeast Asia using mobile phones, while New Yorkers can get only partial service on north–south avenues and none at all on east–west cross streets?

On a similar note, if you decide to climb Mount Everest in the Himalayas, a Nepali telecommunications firm offers 3G service all the way to the summit, which gives you access to high-speed Internet and video calls using a mobile phone. I don't know if they have a tower on top or a Sherpa covered in tinfoil with a wire hanger sticking out of his pack, but either way, be careful when backing up to show Mom the panoramic view.

Technology is even having a positive impact on the traffic situation in India. Concerned citizens are posting pictures of rule breakers on Facebook, which the police monitor and use to issue tickets. Interestingly, a percentage of those photographed violating traffic laws are police officers who are *not* in pursuit of renegade drivers and are left to prove that they were somehow involved in official police business. If you think you were framed, it's possible to appeal and get a hearing. Just don't take photos and create postings while driving since that's also illegal.

India currently has the fastest-growing economy of any democracy, or "democrazy" as it is sometimes known, due to the chaos that accompanies progress on such a massive scale. In the 1990s, the country began moving away from socialism and toward a free-market economy. Since then, there's been a decline in agricultural output but substantial growth in the service industry, which includes banking, communication, and particularly information technology, with the rise of companies such as Infosys, HCL, Wipro, and Tata Consultancy Services. It's home to world-class universities like Hyderabad's Indian School of Business, top-drawer medical facilities such as Mumbai's Kokilaben Dhirubhai Ambani Hospital, and sprawling corporate campuses like the one operated by Infosys in Bangalore. For those who can afford it, there are modern shopping malls selling international brands, dozens of new high-end hotels, neatly manicured suburban enclaves, fancy restaurants, fast-food chains, espresso bars, private schools, luxury cars, and toll highways. If that's not enough, Starbucks has just announced that they're on the way to rescue Indians from reasonably priced coffee and chai.

A Delhi metro system, which is being built in phases, now has more than 120 stations plus links to airports. Residents are so thrilled with their subway that riders volunteer to police the cars for spitting, littering, sitting on the floor, or any other antisocial passenger behavior. As a result, the system remains clean and pleasant, a great source of pride, and already has its own museum at the Patel Chowk station.

Another transportation revolution is under way in the shape of the Tata Nano, a rear-engine four-passenger automobile billed as the world's smallest (and cheapest) car. The Tata Nano, manufactured in India, and not to be confused with the iPod nano, will provide families currently packing five on a scooter with a substantial upgrade. I test-drove one of these tiny wonders in Mumbai (I was test-driven, is more accurate) and it's amazing—an actual four-seat automobile with incredible suspension (to handle India's bone-rattling roads), air-conditioning, radio, and cup holders that doesn't feel like a bumper car or golf cart and can be sold fully loaded in your choice of three colors for under three thousand dollars! Just don't ask how Mumbai is going to handle one more automobile on its already cratered and overflowing city streets. As for the rest of the country, thirty-five out of every hundred households in Delhi now own a car and only twelve of every hundred in Calcutta, so there's enormous potential demand if incomes continue to rise and jobs are created.

As a result of so many improvements, the economy has been growing at a rate of more than 9 percent a year and is expected to soon reach 10 percent, while economists predict that India will grow faster than any large country over the next twenty-five years. How can they beat out China, where the government orders fifty thousand miles of tracks to be put down and the following month you've got a world-class railroad? Due to China's one-child policy, the workforce is aging, while India has what's called a demographic dividend, with the ratio of children and old people to working-age adults one of the best in the world. (A check that can only be cashed if India successfully educates these youngsters.) Furthermore, where China's growth has been state directed, India is a country of millions of entrepreneurs with enormous capacity to solve problems through the application of their unlimited creativity, ambition, and imagination. Indians can also say whatever they want about the government without being swept off to jail. Ideas tend to flow more freely in a culture that doesn't insist upon secrecy, censorship, and occasional crackdowns on their own citizenry with tanks and machine guns. (China executes more people in a week than India has since Independence, in 1947.) Protests against corruption that swept the country in 2011 were not crushed by soldiers. Just the opposite. Government officials listened to the people and promised a more intense package of reforms. Indians do not fear their government. In fact, the prevailing attitude, especially in the big cities, is that authority is there to be defied. The abuse that traffic police alone must deal with should be enough to prove that this is the farthest thing from an authoritarian state.

Access to the Internet is unrestricted, and India has a larger circulation of newspapers than any country in the world. There are more than four hundred independent television stations in operation, with more than half concentrating on news. Journalists and tourists in India may go and explore wherever they wish and stop and talk with whomever they like. Despite the fact that this results in a continuous barrage of reports about the growing gap between the haves and have-nots along with land-use disputes, to its great credit, India has nothing to hide.

With numerous plans on board for even better infrastructure, including faster trains, new highways, airports, backup generators, and water-treatment plants, India is hoping to make a successful bid for the Olympics over the next decade or so. The 2010 Commonwealth Games, which gathered athletes from seventy-two nations in New Delhi, got off to a rocky start with schedule delays and accusations of corruption, but most agree it was mainly a success, with India's athletes also performing well. Maybe there's room for both sports and premed classes, after all!

As for what seem like endless charges of casual corruption amidst a tangled bureaucracy, the computerization of information such as landholdings and individual work histories, along with a number of new laws enacted to empower the citizenry, is making it easier for individuals to navigate government services and secure pensions. These changes are taking the form of a Better Business Bureau, which forces officials to clean up their acts now that ordinary citizens can access records, file complaints, and seek redress for being overcharged or stonewalled. A law protecting whistleblowers is also in the works. Websites such as I Paid A Bribe allow victims to anonymously report any government officials or service providers who ask that palms be greased, and for what, without fear of retaliation. Meantime, programs to help the poor are employing local village watchdogs to make sure that *all* of the funds reach their proper destination. On the downside, the man appointed by the government to head India's anticorruption task force was recently forced by the Supreme Court to resign when faced with charges of corruption.

As a large multiethnic democracy, India has much in common with the United States. However, the subcontinent is often called a salad bowl as opposed to a melting pot, because so many different languages, faiths, and cultures maintain their separate places in a large, liberated society. Throughout the ages, the mystique of India has inspired journeys by Alexander the Great, Marco Polo, Vasco da Gama, the Beatles, and beat poet Allen Ginsberg. It's the world's most famous destination for pilgrims—religious, spiritual, and otherwise—wanting maladies healed, heartaches cured, conundrums solved, and demons vanquished. It's where soul searchers check into ashrams looking for enlightenment, much the way American movie stars head to rehab. And I truly believe that Westerners seeking answers can and do find them in India. The wandering scholars of medieval Europe described the double helix of travel and wisdom as *solvitur ambulando*, "It is solved by walking." One quickly comes to see that if you have twenty thousand dollars a year on which to live plus health insurance, then you're very lucky and/or blessed and that fulfillment is about spending time with people you like while enjoying both your work and play. As the Russian writer Aleksandr Solzhenitsyn said, "If you desire to change the world, where would you start? With yourself or others?"

As much as I enjoyed the writing in *Eat, Pray, Love* by Elizabeth Gilbert, with regard to India she said, "Outside the walls of the Ashram, it is all dust and poverty." There's dust and poverty and color and excitement and ingenuity and much, much more. As Mark Twain wrote 110 years earlier, "So far as I am able to judge, nothing has been left undone, either by man or nature, to make India the most extraordinary country that the sun visits on his rounds. Nothing seems to have been forgotten, nothing overlooked."

However, my favorite quote came from a passenger aboard my Air India flight on the way home. The plane was departing New Delhi at midnight, and all of us weary travelers had the same idea—eat Domino's Pizza in the departure lounge, climb aboard the plane, and pass out for twelve hours. But after only three hours, a flight attendant went around waking everyone up for breakfast. There was basically a passenger mutiny, but whereas Americans were just grumpy and muttering oaths, a feisty Indian woman shouted, "Tell me where it is breakfast time—not in India, not in New York! Where? Honolulu?" Alcoholics like to say that it's always five o'clock somewhere, and so perhaps the same can be said about the breakfast hour.

India continues to be a place of contrast and contradiction, where whatever you imagined will probably be proved wrong and you'll eventually find an example of the exact opposite. But what can one expect from a country named after the Indus River, which is now mostly in Pakistan? A place of snake charmers and wandering storytellers, but also of cutting-edge technology and students flocking to medical schools. Where people make pilgrimages to worship goddesses, but girls are often killed in the womb for being female. A landscape so varied as to include snowcapped Himalayas, scorching deserts, placid lakes, vast mustard farms, lush saffron fields, verdant cherry orchards, deep jungle backwaters of rice paddies and coconut groves, dark forests inhabited by tribal villages, southern mountain ranges blanketed with spice gardens and tea plantations, and thousands of miles of white sand beaches? India is said to be the birthplace of chess, navigation, algebra, trigonometry, calculus, martial arts, and the board game Chutes and Ladders (a.k.a. Snakes and Ladders), although other cultures have also staked their claims to these disciplines (except for Chutes and Ladders), similar to the way that more than a dozen outfits in Manhattan claim to be Ray's Pizzeria. (However, one competitor attempted reverse psychology by naming his shop Not Ray's Pizza.)

The largest problem is, of course, poverty on a grand scale. Eight Indian states account for more poor people than the twenty-six poorest African nations combined. I feel particularly guilty about this because I just leased a new Lexus, and apparently they ran out of luxury add-ons and decided to keep our backsides from sweating by blowing cool air out of the seat cushions. People shouldn't be going hungry or suffering from malaria while my butt crack is being electronically cooled. Things were only made worse when I read on the Lexus Internet forum that buyers were actually complaining that their asses weren't cool *enough*, while their backs felt warm and "swampy."

Microlending, the practice of extending very small loans to those in poverty as a way of sparking entrepreneurship, has been enormously successful despite some recent setbacks along the lines of the subprime mortgage crisis in the States. Billionaire venture capitalist Vinod Khosla is turning out to be the Bill

Gates of India, as he applies the laws of commerce to build entities that will provide people with a pathway out of poverty. Khosla backs businesses involved in win/win services, such as making education loans, distributing solar panels in villages, and helping dairy farmers. Azim H. Premji, chairman of the information technology giant Wipro, has started a foundation to improve public primary schools. The Indian conglomerate Tata Group finances numerous research, medical, educational, and cultural institutions. Other Indian businessmen and billionaires (*Forbes* estimates there are now nearly seventy) are following in their footsteps, although somewhat slowly, since the tradition used to be that when you raked in the rupees you raced camels, bought cricket teams, and built big temples. However, several flashy moneymen have recently placed substantial orders at yacht dealerships.

Meantime, the Self-Employed Women's Association of India (SEWA) is a trade union for low-paid female contract workers and entrepreneurs who don't earn salaries or qualify for benefits. Its main goal is to lift women out of poverty through education, access to banking, introduction to technology, and leadership training. Almost 93 percent of all women work outside the organized employment sector and thus lack any sort of job protection or security. SEWA also champions women's rights. In 2006, after a twenty-eight-year-old Muslim woman was raped by her sixty-nine-year-old father-in-law, several Muslim clerics decided that the marriage to her husband, with whom she had five children, should be declared void, and she should marry her father-in-law and treat her husband as her son. After SEWA and other women's groups protested, the father-in-law was instead given a ten-year prison sentence and ordered to pay the woman 8,000 rupees (about $180) in compensation.

India provides the highest number of foreign students to the United States. The South Asian population in the States has grown more than 200 percent since 1990 and now tops 3 million. Meantime, the children who were born in America following the wave of immigration in the mid-1960s have fully assimilated and are a growing force in entertainment, fashion, culinary arts, politics, academia, medicine, entrepreneurship, IT, finance, architecture, and engineering. Why, Indians are even starting to be indicted for insider trading. In fact, it's said the only things preventing one from becoming president are that there's no chance for promotion, and the White House isn't big enough for all of their in-laws. Indian Americans are currently the wealthiest ethnic group in America. Not only that, they are ferocious spellers, so you'd better start brushing up on *definitely* and *separate* if you don't want to be *embarrassed*.

One can only hope that as the Indian economy continues to expand, a rising tide will lift canoes and catamarans and especially lifeboats along with the billionaires' yachts. Whereas 54 percent of the population lived below the poverty line in the 1970s, it is now down to 25 percent. Famines have been largely eradicated. When a drought strikes, food is moved from one place to another by railway, truck, or plane. Government agencies and charities are hard at work implementing solutions. It's possible to make donations to organizations that help clean the water, stamp out disease, feed the poor, and educate children. If you decide to travel to India, your tourist dollars trickle down to help eradicate poverty. While there, if you see a woman selling scarves on the street (the quality is usually very good) and can buy some as presents, this money almost always goes directly toward her household and for schooling her children. Or else make a gift of the money. In a new book called *Just Give Money to the Poor,* three economic development experts argue that donations to relief organizations mostly go for training and development projects with varied results while much of the money is wasted on administration. Meanwhile, money given directly to the poor (with advice on how they should use it) was usually spent sensibly on starting businesses, educating children, and buying fertilizer, seeds, and farm animals. As it turns out, the thing that poor people lack most is money!

Indian TV shows and advertising are beginning to feature more modern lifestyles, such as young people wanting to experiment with dating and/or living alone before marriage. Or a financially independent daughter making her own purchasing decisions. There are even story lines featuring live-in boyfriends and girlfriends and uncommitted couples who flirt with others. Although, in a nod to tradition, there's a reality show called *Perfect Bride* in which mothers select wives for their sons. However, I'm sure it's only a matter of time before an American reality show has audience members voting on spouses for the participants.

Nowadays, Indians are wild about contests—singing, comedy, dancing, personality. Hence, the popularity of *Indian Idol*. "What so appealed to the millions of viewers was not the singing and dancing itself, but the ruthless fairness that the shows suggested," writes Anand Giridharadas in *India Calling: An Intimate Portrait of a Nation's Remaking*. "For many, life in India had not been very fair. So many spheres had required a connection or a bribe or a favor: getting into a school, getting a job, getting the apartment you loved. The competition shows resonated because they suggested the coming of a new world in which everyone would have their chance to sing, and the market would judge, and the best would truly win."

The Internet is also doing its part to introduce older generations to modern lifestyles. It's possible to educate oneself on various topics without the entire family knowing about it. And as we've discovered in

America, forwarding to older relatives jokey e-mails and cute animal videos that accidentally result in them receiving ads for penile enlargements, vaginal rejuvenation, and Viagra is a great way of breaking down communication barriers.

Interestingly, I noticed many more smiles on India's poor than I find on residents of Park Avenue apartment buildings in New York City. If you ask ministers whether they'd rather counsel the rich or the poor, they'll usually answer the rich, since wealthy individuals know that money doesn't solve most problems. One can also argue that the fewer possessions you own, the less you have to worry about. Likewise, the more goods you have, the more you have to lose. Ideally, everyone on the planet should have what they need plus discretionary income, but endless desire can be a source of suffering that leaves the financially blessed poor and distressed.

I found that drug addiction and violent crime were much lower in India than in the West. The prisons are not overflowing. Yes, there's a Mafia, actually several, but you tend not to get gang-related drive-by shootings, and entire towns aren't being lost to methamphetamine addiction. Funnily enough, the general populace is just as spellbound by the hookups and breakdowns of their Bollywood stars as we are by the shenanigans of our own tinsel town royalty. However, people are not as quick to anger as they are in the West, especially in a city like

Manhattan, where natives regularly become enraged over perceived slights and petty injustices. (Okay, I yelled "We all paid for a ticket!" at a well-dressed man who jumped the line to get on the ferry in Mumbai, but I hate cutters, and they claim the country is a democracy.)

In an Indian slum, strangers are welcomed and even shown hospitality. At the very worst, they're left unmolested. In an American slum, this tends not to be the case. My own experience as an American in a number of bad neighborhoods throughout the United States is that residents view my presence warily, want to know what business I have there, and make it clear that I'd best be on my way. A foreigner would certainly have an even worse time.

From the point of view of world politics, the most stunning story that India currently has to tell is what happens when women are on their way to fully participating in a democratic society. The most poverty-stricken nations are dictatorships and theocracies where women remain down-at-heel. These countries are suppressing a full 50 percent of their talent, creativity, and potential and will continue to flounder until their women are no longer subjugated. India's rise has proven that educating girls and empowering women can be the most successful antipoverty campaign known to man.

Bangladesh, which was a part of India before Partition and practically synonymous with starvation in the latter half of the twentieth century, has over the past fifteen years transitioned from being one of the poorest countries on earth to maintaining a strong economy and reducing poverty by 20 percent. This is largely the result of educating girls and women and making them productive partners in a secular and democratic society. No more star-studded famine fund-raiser concerts for the Bangladeshis, thanks all the same.

As a bonus, when development from the ground up leads to more opportunity and prosperity all around, citizens are less likely to become radicalized and involved in terrorism. When a young person has hope and dignity and the prospect of a bright future, living is viewed as more meaningful than dying for a cause, whatever it might be. The biggest threat to any society is the creation of citizens who have nothing to lose.

During my trip to India, I did not practice yoga in Yamuna Nagar, levitate in Lucknow, consult an herbal healer in Hamirpir, receive a mantra from a Mahabubnagar yogi, find inner peace in Irinjalakuda, study Vishistadvaita philosophy in Firozabad, have mind-altering experiences in Ashok Nagar, or leave offerings at the altars of Annapurna. Instead, I saw a lot of human nature, which I believe helps a person decide what kind of human being he or she would like to be, and that was indeed a benediction.

I left India thinking how clever I'd been to avoid a swine flu epidemic, dysentery, leprosy, dengue fever, tuberculosis, and malaria, which was rampant during the monsoon season, along with a new superbug that had started in the subcontinent and was rapidly spreading throughout the world as a result of medical tourism. However, when I arrived back in Manhattan, there was a raging bedbug infestation and a number of public places were closed, including a Times Square movie theater and several large retail outlets. The bedbug czar appeared on TV to report that the city was under siege and losing the war on bedbugs. Meantime, the Long Island Railroad had collapsed due to equipment failure, with Amtrak's northeast corridor following right behind since they share tracks and switches, thus stranding thousands of travelers. In other news, half a billion eggs had been recalled due to salmonella poisoning, while several high-ranking politicians were facing corruption charges. Perhaps I should've stayed in India. As the New York State Lottery ads prophetically remind us, "Hey, you never know."

About the Author

© Denise Winters

Laura Pedersen is a former *New York Times* columnist and the best-selling author of ten books, including the award-winning humorous memoir *Buffalo Gal*. She has appeared on The Oprah Winfrey Show, Late Night with David Letterman, Good Morning America, The Today Show, Primetime Live, CNN, Fox News, and MSNBC. More information can be found at www .LauraPedersenBooks.com.